Violence

D1214982

JACQUES ELLUL

Violence

Reflections

from a Christian Perspective

TRANSLATED BY CECELIA GAUL KINGS

MOWBRAYS

LONDON & OXFORD

© 1969 The Seabury Press, Incorporated

First published in the U.K. by SCM, London

This edition published 1978
by A. R. Mowbray & Co. Ltd.,
Saint Thomas House, Becket Street, Oxford OX1 1SJ

ISBN 0 264 66530 9

Printed in Great Britain by
Billing & Sons Limited
Guildford, London and Worcester

Contents

Violence

1

Traditional Views

THE CHURCHES and the theologians, it is helpful to recall at the outset, have never been in unanimous agreement in their views on violence in human society. Today most people believe that general opinion in the past accepted and, in one way or other, blessed the state's use of violence and condemned any revolt against the ruling authorities. But it is a mistake to assume that it is only in our day that Christians have adopted a nonviolent stance or, on the other hand, have ranged themselves on the side of revolutionary violence. These two attitudes have had their representatives, their theologians, their sects from the beginning. Let us then put the problem in perspective by reviewing, briefly, the main facts concerning these several positions.

COMPROMISE

As early as the end of the first century, the Christians found themselves under a political power—the Roman empire—which persecuted them but at the same time insured a kind of order and a kind of justice. They also found themselves confronting biblical passages which affirmed the value

1

of the state—or, at the very least, of the official political authorities—and ascribed to it a divine origin. We shall not
here take up the innumerable exegeses of Romans 13 and
parallel texts. The important thing is to understand that
such passages and exegeses predisposed the Christians to accept the political power as more or less valid. On the practical level, however, they saw that the state always threatened to become a persecuting state, and they saw also that it
used violence against its enemies, internal or external. For
war certainly seemed violence pure and simple, and the
police operated by violence—the crucifixion of thousands of
slaves, for instance. How then accept that, when it used such
methods, this power was ordained by God? To be sure, the
Christians understood that the state legitimately wields the
sword. But was this valid in all circumstances?

Questions like these led to the development of various theological positions—that, for instance, which was to be dominant in the West during the Middle Ages (so-called political
Augustinianism), or that which triumphed at Byzantium.
What is remarkable in these theological constructions is that
they do not retain the biblical perspective which sees the
state as ordained by God, in harmony with the divine order,
and at the same time as the Beast of the Abyss, the Great
Babylon; as wielder of the sword to chastise the wicked and
protect the good, but also as the source of persecution and injustice. Instead of maintaining the balance of both these
truths, these theologians chose rather to validate the political
power a priori on a global scale. They worked out their position on the basis of a kind of monism. The question they put
was: Under what conditions is the state just, and when does
it cease to be just? This led to casuistic reasoning on the acts
of the state, and presently to the elaboration of a compromise which allowed the Christian and the church to live in
the situation where they found themselves.

Very quickly the state became the auxiliary of the church, and vice versa. The emperor was declared "outside bishop," and the state became the secular arm carrying out the decisions of the church. For its part, the church became an earthly magnitude with a political calling. The world was divided between two powers, the spiritual and the temporal. Nevertheless the church continued to claim for itself the right of judging the state. It was she who declared whether or not the state was just. She could pronounce condemnations, and actually went so far as to order the deposition of the prince. She could do no more than speak the truth about the state. It must be admitted that under this "Christian" regime she often used her power of truth-speaking for her own advantage, to defend her goods and her personages. But justice requires us to recognize that she also used it to protect the weak and to establish peace among the powerful. Contrary to general opinion, the church's struggle for these ends was very successful in the Middle Ages. Nevertheless the political power, though recognized, limited, and in some measure controlled, continued to use violence.

The theologians and the canonists, leaning on the Roman tradition, then established positions which are still influential today. As regards violence, three main points were advanced. First, as to internal violence, the reasoning soon took shape as follows: The state is not of the same nature as man; therefore, since it has received the sword from the hand of God, it never acts by violence when it constrains, condemns and kills. Next, a distinction was made between violence and force: The state is invested with force; it is an organism instituted and ordained by God, and remains such even when it is unjust; even its harshest acts are not the same thing as the angry or brutal deed of the individual. The individual surrenders to his passions, he commits violence. The state—even the corrupt state—obeys quite different promptings; even in its demonization (as Karl Barth was also to say) it still, negatively, does God's will. It is the institution which demonstrates the difference between violence and force. The theologian Suarez's statement of the matter is well known: a man cannot lawfully kill his neighbor, nor can two men together, nor a hundred men, nor ten thousand; but a judge can lawfully pronounce a sentence of death. There is the difference. This indisputably legitimate power derives from the nature of the state; that nature does not reside in man. There is all the difference between violence and force.

But this was not the end of the matter, for, obviously, the state is not necessarily just, not necessarily right. So the next question arose: whether the state itself is just or not; for the power that condemns to death (and has the right to do so!) evidently may be tyrannical or oppressive, or may condemn by mistake. The question then becomes one of whether the state makes just laws or not. And it is the spiritual power which can say whether those laws are just. (Calvin himself adopted this casuistry.) A further question is whether the prince acquired his power by just procedures or simply seized it by violence; if the latter, he is a tyrant and unjust. Nevertheless the power he holds renders his sentences valid, without violence. Moreover, if the prince uses justly the power he seized by violent means, it is legitimized in the end. Then the final question: whether the state's use of force conforms to the laws. Here again we find that confidence in the institution which marked ancient Rome: a death sentence pronounced according to previously established procedures, for a crime previously defined as such, and in application of existing laws—that sentence is just. All the state can do is make decisions in conformity with its laws. (Except that sometimes the laws themselves may be unjust; whether they are is up to the church to decide.) In any case, force is just when its use conforms to the laws; when it does not conform to the laws, it is still force—not violence—but unjust force.

In all these matters, too, Calvin generally, though with some nuances, took the positions that were widely held in his time. We today hold many of these ideas, even if we have abandoned the conceptions of the church as judge of the state and of the supremacy of the spiritual over the temporal power. Yet modern Christians are always prone to judge the state and to tell it what it ought to do—thus tacitly admitting that the state is valid, legitimate, and a priori capable of using force justly.

By such a course of reasoning, the theologians and canonists attempted, first, to clear the state of the charge of violence by explaining that it was not violence; and second, to establish a viable compromise between the state and Christians.

The same method was applied to the second form of violence; namely, war. Obviously the political authority was always fighting with its external enemies. It waged war. Should it have done so? Very soon—as early as 314, at the Council of Arles—the church realized that to deny the state the right to go to war was to condemn it to extinction. But the state is ordained by God; therefore it must have the right to wage war. Yet is not war intolerable violence?

So began the casuistry of the just war. To analyze the successive phases of that argumentation and to describe the tests set up would be superfluous. Let us simply recall the climactic point of the just-war debate in the analysis made by Gratian and Thomas Aquinas, which became the traditional doctrine of the Catholic Church.* It is based on the conviction that man can retain control of violence, that violence can be kept in the service of order and justice and even

---

* B. de Solages, *La théorie de la juste guerre* (Paris, 1956).

of peace, that violence is good or bad depending on the use or purpose it is put to.

Clearly the theologians' prescriptions for a just war have theoretical solidity. According to them seven conditions must coincide to make a war just: the cause fought for must itself be just; the purpose of the warring power must remain just while hostilities go on; war must be truly the last resort, all peaceful means having been exhausted; the methods employed during the war to vanquish the foe must themselves be just; the benefits the war can reasonably be expected to bring for humanity must be greater than the evils provoked by the war itself; victory must be assured; the peace concluded at the end of the war must be just and of such nature as to prevent a new war.

Obviously we need not, in this brief historical review, proceed to analyze or criticize this elaboration of the just-war idea. Let us point out only that the whole argument rests on the concept of "justice"—a concept that was perhaps clear to the Middle Ages but certainly is not so today; moreover in those times notions of "justice" were much more juridical and Aristotelian than Christian. Let us point out also that these seven conditions were formulated in a day when it was possible to see a war situation with relative clarity; but the phenomena of modern war—total war as well as wars of subversion—and the extent of the battlefields rule out utterly the *application* of these seven criteria and render them altogether inoperative.

Nevertheless these just-war ideas have been taken up again and again. At present we find three orientations. Catholic thought generally poses the problem in terms of the lesser evil: war is legitimate as an extreme means of preventing greater evil for humanity. But note that this greater evil is variously identified—by some, as the spread of communism; by others, as the exploitation of the Third World by the capitalist nations. Karl Barth takes over the idea of a just war. But of the conditions set up by the medieval theologians, he considers the third the sole test—that of the *ultima ratio.* Granted that the state cannot be condemned to disappear, its right to defend itself must also be granted—but not unless it has previously employed every means to solve the difference pacifically, has made every possible sacrifice and exhausted every possible procedure for a peaceful settlement. That is to say, war cannot be just except as a last resort.

Barth's view also seems unsatisfactory. The fact is that such negotiations and efforts for peace often give the eventual aggressor time to prepare himself better. For example, we must admit that the Munich pact of 1938, or the nonintervention in Italy's war against Ethiopia in 1935, bespoke wise and just attitudes on the part of France and England; and yet it was precisely these settlements that made the war of 1939-1945 infinitely more savage. All the world knows that if other nations had intervened against Hitler and Mussolini in 1934-1935, those two regimes would have foundered—and millions of lives would have been saved.

Finally, while they generally decline to set up definitions of a "just war," some Christians today state their position as follows: We are forced to go to war; we must accept war because, according to Christian teaching, we must obey the state; but the Christian, as Christian, will engage in war without hating his foes; he will kill the enemy but he will not hate him. In this connection there has been talk about the "Christian paradox"; for to love the enemy and at the same time act cruelly toward him seems impossible. I do not say that this is absolutely impossible. I do say that the heat of battle and the violence of combat rule out any thought or emotion except the consciousness of "kill or be killed." I say also that present-day long-distance weapons, which permit the collective destruction of a far-off enemy, rule out love; what is called "love" in this situation will be mere sentimentality, and its expression mere verbalism.

But above all we must recall that the attitude described above, which seems so modern, is a very old one. The Catholic Church, for example, held this attitude toward heretics. She condemned the heretic not to punish him but to save him, not to protect herself or society against him but to lead him back to the truth; for on the other side of his heresy, as it were, she loved the person she put to death to deliver him from his heresy. I am not being ironical at all. Excommunication was called a *remedium animae*. And the *auto-da-fé*, the act of faith, was meant for the salvation of the condemned. It is easy to see where such a doctrine can lead.

The last point developed by the medieval theologians is this: that if the violence used by the state is force, hence legitimate (even if sometimes unjust), and if the state is eminently a servant of God, any revolt against it is forbidden. Some kinds of opposition to the state may be allowed; for example, the church, as we have seen, may be competent to oppose the state. Calvin holds that the "officials" may offer opposition, but this must always be reasoned, measured, juridical opposition. On the one hand, the subject himself may absolutely not rise up against the state; on the other hand, the methods of opposition may never be violent. But the individual's opposition will *always*, inevitably, be violent, therefore must be condemned. *Coup d'état*, rebellion, all this kind of thing is rejected by the theologians. Since the authorities (and there are many definitions of "authorities," but they all lead to the same conclusion in the end) in power are ordained by God, every revolt is a revolt against God himself. This was also the position of Calvin and Luther. As to Calvin, everyone knows that he attacked the revolutionaries, "those ferocious beasts," and considered any tyranny, no matter how harsh, better than the disorder of revolt. As to

Luther, everyone knows what stand he took at the time of the peasant war. In fact, in this line of thought, when a man uses violence the state has a right to apply all measures against him.

But this theological orientation, which may be considered the dominant one, seems like a solution of compromise. The reasoning back of it, one may suppose, ran something like this: "We certainly have to live in society. These are no longer the days of the first Christian generation, when extreme, uncompromising attitudes were possible. We must accommodate ourselves to the situation that exists; we must become a part of it if we are to go on living. Now there is a political power in this society, and it often plays a positive role. It is better to normalize that power and to parley with it. It is better to round off the angles of Christian demands and to seek solutions of compromise, thus preserving the church and giving the state a new meaning." Such reasoning led to over-evaluation of the several positive texts in the Epistles which uphold the political power. This position has generally been defended by theologians and church people and by the men at the heart of the ecclesiastical institution.

NONVIOLENCE

Opposed to the position described above is that of nonviolence. This, too, is an orientation that goes back to the beginnings of Christianity and has always been represented in the church. It seems to witness to the teaching of Jesus on the level of personal relations—Love your enemy, turn the other cheek. Jesus carried the commandment "Thou shalt not kill" to the extreme limit, and in his person manifested nonviolence and even nonresistance to evil. When he was arrested, he neither allowed Peter to defend him nor called the "twelve legions of angels" to his aid. But this is common

knowledge. In any case, it seems that up to the fourth century, such was the view of Christians generally and the official position of the church, in regard to both public affairs
and, especially, military service.* To be sure, the first and
succeeding generations obeyed and honored the political
power, but, because of their love of humanity and their respect for the stranger, they refused to render military service. Indeed they showed their horror of war plainly. In this
connection the testimony of Lactantius (*Divine Institutions*)
is most important because of both its incisiveness and the
character of the witness-bearer.

The refusal of Christians to render military service, then,
was prompted by their desire to go beyond the simple local
community and extend it to embrace all men. Nevertheless
there probably were Christians in the army, though no text
or inscription earlier than the end of the second century
clearly indicates as much. Tertullian is the first author to
mention the presence of Christians in the military, and he
condemns it. The writings of his era indicate that Christians
became soldiers only under duress, and that soldiering was
not approved of. Then, as the military needs of the empire
grew in the third and fourth centuries, the conflict broke out.
In Africa, toward the end of the third century, many Christians were martyred because they refused to serve in the
armies. Best known is the case of Maximilian, whose words
have become famous: "I cannot be a soldier, I cannot do evil,
because I am a Christian." Others at first accepted military
service, then, plagued by conscience, either deserted or suf-
fered martyrdom in consequence of their faith. Among the
Copts, too, it was the Christians who started the conflict.
Likewise in Gaul, the most celebrated case there being that

---

* For what follows, I have drawn on the excellent historical study by
J. M. Hornus, *Évangile et Labarum* (Geneva: Labor & Fides, 1960).

of St. Martin of Tours, who, a soldier and a soldier's son, after his conversion refused to serve any longer and accepted
death, explaining his position in terms that, theologically, are
remarkable.

It seems then that—granted its varied origins—the stand
for nonviolence was taken by a great many Christians, though
certainly not by all. But in the fourth century this position
became less rigid. The last military martyrs no longer objected to army service as such; they only refused to fight
against Christians.

Officially, the church also seems to have gone along with
condemnation of the army in that period. Not only Tertullian
but Clement of Alexandria and the document called "Apos-
tolic Tradition" (Roman ecclesiastical regulations dating
from the end of the second century) declare that he who
holds the sword must cast it away and that if one of the
faithful becomes a soldier he must be rejected by the church,
"for he has scorned God." However, this official stand was
soon relaxed. It was agreed that the ordinary soldier who was
converted while in the military might remain a soldier, but
that the officer would have to give up his rank. Apparently
this remained the official position until the fourth century.
But little by little extenuating circumstances were recognized. For example, it was admitted that the Christian who
is forced by the public authorities to become a soldier should
not be condemned. Also, a distinction was made between
militare and *bellare*: in time of peace the Christian might be
a soldier (*militare*), but in time of war he must refuse to fight
(*bellare*). The Synod of Elvira and then the Council of Nicea
authorized these relaxations. Thus the principle that the
Christian must not be a soldier was maintained, with certain
modifications and tolerances. And it seems that the principle
was consistently applied. In fact it accounts for one of the accusations leveled against the Christians by Celsus: by run-

ning away from military service and refusing to defend the empire and their country, they greatly weaken the army and prove themselves enemies of mankind.

This position was abandoned at the time of Constantine's conversion. Indeed, after the Council of Arles, Christians were required to serve in the army, and Augustine became the grand theorist of the necessity of defending the earthly city. But the belief that Christians must refuse to do violence persists in the church to this day. Conscientious objection to military service is, after all, only a specific illustration of this position. Need I mention Francis of Assisi and his refusal to do violence even to animals? The story of the wolf of Gubbio is particularly significant. And the astonishing success of the Franciscan movement, which was based on the principle of nonviolence, demonstrates that this "evangelical sweetness" carried a permanent appeal for the people of the church. This was also the principle of the Brothers of Waldo (at Lyons) and of those heretical movements—Joachimites, Brothers of the Poor Life, etc.—which preached true evangelical communism, practiced absolute nonviolence, and declared that apocalyptic visions had revealed that the "poor and pure religious orders will bring in the mystical government of the world." But these ideas were not altogether pure, for by calling for the exaltation of the poor they implied condemnation of the rich. In time, members of these movements abandoned the ideal of sweetness and plunged into violent struggle against the rich. John of Leyden is a striking example. He, too, declared for nonviolence and spiritual, evangelical communism, and in the end he resorted to violence in defense of his "city of saints."

Finally, this orientation became very strong in the church after the war of 1914, when conscientious-objection and nonviolent movements multiplied everywhere. Some churches adopted this position—for example, certain Baptist churches, the Pentecostalists, Jehovah's Witnesses. In France, the Reformed Church acknowledged that conscientious objection is a vocation in the church, a prophetic sign.

But it is important to note that proponents of nonviolence differed among themselves. Some held that "Thou shalt not kill" is an absolute commandment, admitting of no exceptions; that this is a law of God which applies unconditionally to and against everyone. Others believed that the objective was above all to seek out ways of expressing love. Hence the view developed that in and of itself, as absolute act, nonviolence is of no direct value; that the principle of nonviolence must lead to ways of acting that are valid expressions of authentic love of neighbor. Thus there is no need to distinguish between good and bad, oppressor or aggressor; violence must not be used against them, because violence is necessarily contrary to love. Love can overcome evil, and we are under an imperative to go beyond the order of justice by way of the order of love. This line of thought, however, rests on the conviction that it is God who transforms the heart of man. In other words, it betokens an attitude of utter faith in the action of the Holy Spirit, a recognition that the will of God is not accomplished through violence on the part of man, but on the contrary that man's obedience, sacrifice and nonresistance to evil clear the way for the action of God to manifest itself.

This attitude leads to two approaches. The first centers on the person of the proponent of nonviolence. Nonviolence, it declares, cannot be an "external" attitude; it resides in the heart of man. It is in being himself at peace that a man becomes peaceful; it is in living the love of God that he becomes capable of manifesting that love; it is through his practice of it in his personal life that nonviolence spreads to society. A man who believed in nonviolence yet remained violent in character would count for nothing and his action would be meaningless.

The second approach centers on the military and its grow-ing power.* In our society, adherents of this view point out, every kind of violence is dealt with, ultimately, by the army or the police. An oppressive or unjust government can remain in power only because it has armed force at its disposal. Therefore the army is the point at which the issue must be joined. For, stripped of armed support, an unjust, oppressive government or social order can save itself only by mending its ways. Thus the whole problem of nonviolence comes down to this: the state must be divested of its instruments of vio-lence; and, for their part, proponents of nonviolence must respond to the state's use of violence by nonviolent actions— acceptance of sacrifice, noncooperation, civil disobedience, etc. Some hold that the response must be absolutely nonvio-lent; others think that perfect nonviolence is a fiction and that some compromise may be necessary. They put their case in familiar terms: "Of course a person can accept violence and injustice for himself and hold to nonviolence when he alone is affected. But what when another is threatened? Must we not help the victim of oppression? And on the so-cial level, is it not the fact that refusal to act violently against oppressors and to defend the oppressed is to give injustice a free hand, therefore to side with the oppressor? In other words does not this refusal amount to being violent by 'pas-sivity'—but with a good conscience?"

So some proponents of nonviolence argue. But for a long time now these same criticisms have been coming from other quarters also. And in attempting to answer these criticisms pacifists invariably refer to Gandhi and his experience. Ob-viously it is a fact that it was by absolute nonviolence—even amid the crying problems India faced after her liberation—

* On all these problems, see P. Régamey, *Nonviolence et conscience chrétienne*, 1958. English edition, *Nonviolence and the Christian Conscience* (New York: Herder & Herder, 1966).

that Gandhi finally secured not only his country's independence, but led it to adopt policies that no other of the world's
nations will imitate. Certainly this is the fact. But those who
cite this fact forget an essential factor in Gandhi's success.
To whom was his nonviolent approach directed? On the one
hand, to a people shaped by centuries of concern for holi-
ness and the spiritual, a people with highly developed conceptions of virtue and purity—a people, in short, uniquely
capable of understanding and accepting his message. Elsewhere in the world the situation is quite different. On the
other hand, Gandhi was dealing with an invader—Great
Britain—that officially declared itself a Christian nation,
though there is no doubt that it took over India by violence,
corruption, conquest, etc. Yet, because its Christian tradition
was relatively strong, Britain could not remain insensible to
Gandhi's preachment of nonviolence. Even if Britain's affirmation of "Christian values" was merely formal, the affirmation was made, and appealing to it was truly to put the
English government on the spot. If worse came to worst, it
could imprison Gandhi; but it could not simply crush or si-
lence him, and it could not kill his disciples.

But put Gandhi into the Russia of 1925 or the Germany of
1933. The solution would be simple: after a few days he
would be arrested and nothing more would be heard of him.
It was their "Christian liberalism" and their democratic scruples that enabled the English people to sympathize with
nonviolence. Let us entertain no illusions as to what would
have happened elsewhere. But this is exactly the mistake
that proponents of nonviolence so often make. They do not
recognize that India's case is unique. To believe that these
methods would work in all situations is tantamount to believing (1) that a government can maintain itself without ever
using violence and (2) that there is such a thing as a "just
state" which would be sufficient unto itself. Their concern to

show that their position is *also* efficacious lands pacifists in a position that, ultimately, is completely unrealistic. They would do better to declare the validity of nonviolence without pretending that it is universally applicable.

This position has generally been upheld by the "spirituals," the prophets; that is to say, by relatively isolated persons, at least in the beginning. Note, however, that this doctrine influenced church opinion more and more between the two world wars and again after the Second World War. Certainly the example and preaching of proponents of nonviolence have changed the point of view of a great many Christians. Today it is almost unthinkable that a Christian nation should adopt the slogan *"Gott mit uns"* (inscribed on the belt buckle of the German soldiers in 1914). Today no one believes in a "Christian war" or a war to defend Christianity (the last time that idea was exploited was in 1940-41, by the Vichy government); no one believes that God is with "our" armies.

Unfortunately, however, in recent years nonviolence has become selective, that is, politicized. In France, for instance, pacifists have taken a stand in relation to political affairs. They protested nonviolently against the French war in Algeria, but ignored the violences committed by the National Liberation Front. They protested nonviolently against American intervention in Vietnam, but ignored the violences committed by the Viet Cong and gave no thought to the consequences for the whole of Vietnam should a communist government gain control. Yet it is well known that violences have been committed in the north (especially against the Vietnamese Catholics) and that after communist rule was established in North Vietnam its atrocities claimed more victims than were claimed by the actual war.* In other words, if the pacifist becomes involved without being parti-

---

* It must however be recognized that one of France's noblest champions of nonviolence, Pastor Jean Lasserre, maintains a cool head and his objectivity in the midst of all the conflicts and passions.

san, his nonviolence remains authentic; in the contrary case, nonviolence becomes a means of propaganda.

VIOLENCE

Let us now consider a third orientation in Christian thought, an orientation that, like the preceding, has never had official status but has always been represented—albeit in sporadic fashion—in spite of official disapproval. This is the view that, aside from any question of authority, violence on the part of the individual may be legitimate. This is not at all a modern discovery, though the "theologians of revolution" seem to think so. In fact, however, the use of violence, whether by Christians or non-Christians, has always been accepted in Christian thought, on various grounds.

Apparently, the first to act on this idea were the anchorites of the Nile valley, those hairy, savage hermits of the third and fourth centuries, who periodically descended on the great cities of the valley (especially Alexandria) and, wielding their long gnarled sticks, set about beating up people and smashing everything in sight. As they saw it, theirs was a kind of purifying violence. In the face of the corruption of morals rampant in Egypt at that time, they proclaimed the imminence of the stern judgment of God, and drove home their proclamation by their violent actions. They took it upon themselves to punish sinners here and now and to manifest God's judgment on the world in concrete ways. Thus these terrible anchorites were motivated primarily by a prophetic and spiritual concern. They took their cue from the celebrated biblical passage which tells how Jesus whipped the merchants and drove them from the temple.°

But in time the outlook changed completely, and the

° J. Lasserre interprets this text to exclude every and any act of violence on Jesus' part: *I. Cahiers de la réconciliation*, Paris, 1967.

problem became that of the violence of the poor and oppressed against their oppressors. Was such violence legitimate before God? The answer was an unqualified "yes,"
sweeping aside all the Old Testament passages which indicate that God is the one who avenges the misery of the poor
and the suffering of the oppressed; sweeping aside also the
New Testament passages which counsel the unfortunate to
practice the virtue of patience and exhort servants to obey
their masters even if the master is unjust. All these passages
are so familiar that I need not cite chapter and verse here.
But I must emphasize at once that practically no biblical
text directly justifies this "yes."

Note now some of the important applications of this
"yes." Especially significant is Thomas Aquinas' statement
that when a poor person, out of his need, steals, he is not
committing a sin and should not be punished by the church.
The bread he stole was *due* him from the rich man; and if
the poor man stole, it was because of the rich man's hardness
of heart. This analysis of Aquinas' was to be one of the arguments regularly cited to justify violence.

In this connection, reference must be made also to the innumerable social movements that—generally basing their
appeal on Christian grounds—agitated Europe's peasantry
in the Middle Ages. As an example I mention only the movement of Joachim of Floris and its consequences. One element
in Joachim's thought was exaltation of the poor. To be sure,
he meant this on the theoretical level, but the idea was soon
interpreted in a social sense. Wealth came to be viewed as a
crime. The "fury of the proletariat" boiled up from the religious underground. Then, under the leadership of Fra
Dolcino, the Joachimite movement became egalitarian and
violent. Dolcino headed a band of the Illuminated who
plundered and destroyed and announced the reign of the
Spirit. In 1507 they were vanquished by the "forces of order"

—that is, an army commanded by the Bishop of Vercueil. Later on, this kind of thing was repeated again and again.* The sixteenth century particularly saw an ever increasing glorification of violence on the basis of Christian motifs. There was first the great revolt of Thomas Münzer, which aimed to establish a truly Christian state where all would be equal; for, Münzer declared, the children of God are entitled to happiness in this world and to full enjoyment of all the goods of Nature which God gives to man; and they are kept from enjoying what is rightfully theirs by the rich and powerful who have cornered the goods of the world. Münzer's views derived from Reformation ideas, but he was also affected by the spirit of revolt that stirred in the German peasants during most of the fifteenth century. He took Upper Suabia and installed a perfectly egalitarian regime at Mühlhausen. The rich were required to support the poor, and all citizens were forced to observe a strict and simple moral code. Subsequently Münzer reworked his manifesto ("Sorrows and Sufferings of the Poor") into twelve articles. But little by little the Christian, religious substance of his message and preaching was weakened, and in time his movement became a revolt pure and simple, full of hatred and a passion for looting. Meanwhile the former Cistercian monk Heinrich Pfeiffer had joined the movement. But far from bringing into it a more profound element, Pfeiffer's presence only inflamed the passions of the citizens. Be that as it may, when the last battle was fought the peasants were still praying to the Holy Spirit.

The Anabaptist movement was important also in the Low Countries, where John of Leyden, by equally violent means, set up his regime at Münster. Here, too, we find the same

---

* I omit mention of the Crusades, for these were, in the main, conducted under the auspices of the church.

preaching—a mixture of Christian elements (Blessed are the poor. . . . There will be neither rich nor poor), millenarist ideas (we must establish the Kingdom of God on earth at once, for the reign of the Spirit is at hand), and purely social, revolutionary factors. But to say that all this resulted from human misery and that the Christian preachment was simply the ideological veil of the situation is to misjudge the facts. The reverse is the case: the Christian preachment comes first, effectively reaching the hearts of men and stirring them up; and their misery occasions their revolt.* Still, the means used is the same; namely, violence. And, curiously enough, in these movements physical violence often accompanies proclamations of the reign of the Spirit, a reign erupting in violence, as though spiritual passion were incarnated in violence. Remarkable passages in the sermons of John of Leyden testify to this view. For instance, he speaks of the power of the Spirit, and, referring to his enemies, adds: "Terrify them!" Or he quotes the Bible and incites to violence in the same breath: "Don't return for your coat; arm yourselves and follow me!"

Soon after there appeared on the scene another group of Christians who took a stand for violence—not, like the Anabaptists, as a means of relieving the oppressed and improving society, but as a political tool. These were the doctrinaires who posed the problem of the "unjust prince" and tyrannicide. Must the people support a tyrant without protest? A great many writings on this theme are extant, some by jurists or historians—who tried to associate their position with a Christian point of view—others by politicians. I cite two examples. The first is *Vindiciae contra Tyrannos* (1573), about whose author little is known. However, he begins with

---

* Gabriel d'Aubarède (*La révolution des saints,* Paris, 1946) is right in emphasizing that Münster went from *heresy* (first) to *revolt* (second).

a description of the king's function, goes on to explain the double contract between God and king and between king and people, and concludes that if the head of state is a tyrant who has won his office by violence, his subjects are duty-bound to revolt against him and to use all means to destroy his power. The second example is *De justa abdicatione Henrici III*, written by the "Curé of Paris," Boucher, at the time of the Holy League. Boucher plainly defends tyrannicide in principle. But he distinguishes among tyrants, as follows: If the prince is a tyrant by reason of the origin of his power (usurpation, violence): in this case, every citizen has the duty of killing him. If the prince is a tyrant by reason of the abuses of power he commits against the "republic": in this case, the people's representatives must pronounce a judgment (secret, of course!), but private persons will have to carry out the sentence (by assassination). Finally, if the tyrant wrongs private persons, they may not avenge themselves; only the whole people, or the "public powers," can revolt. In all these cases the tyrant is a public enemy. These ideas were in fact applied in the assassination of Henry III.

I need hardly point out that Cromwell and the Levellers held similar views. The interesting thing is that here the two currents of thought described earlier in this section join in favoring violence. On the one hand, there were the Christians who affirmed the validity of violence from a political point of view, as a way of fighting tyranny and bringing in a republican form of government or insuring submission to a "constitution." This was the case with Cromwell. On the other hand, there were the Christians who took the part of the poor and affirmed the validity of violence to defend the poor. This was the case with the Levellers. Note that one of the Levellers, John Lilburne, was perhaps the first to set forth a "theology of revolution." He wrote that "the most authentic servants of Christ have always been the worst enemies of tyranny and the oppressor" (*Legitimate Defense*, 1653).

Study of these writings reveals certain facts that apply generally. These Christians actually moved, and rapidly, from an attack on the political powers to an attack on the church; for the church, they thought, was in league with the political powers (and such was indeed often the case). But, for one thing, their ideas were Christian only in a quite vague and general way (so with Overton of Walwyn). And, for another, their attack on the Christian hypocrites who were in league with the political powers soon led them to reject Christianity itself. Broadly speaking, it may be said that the defense of the poor, prompted in the first place by Christian sentiments of solidarity or charity, crowded out all the rest of Christianity and ended in total abandonment of faith, in indifference to the revelation, and in the atheism that appears to be a normal revolutionary position.

Be that as it may. This position was worked out primarily by "political" men. Faith and theology had small part in it and in any case were not the point of departure, the deep motivators. Rather, Christianity served as the justification, the legitimization of this position, as a complementary argument. What interested these people was political or social action. They held that faith or theological arguments might be means, instruments, but never decisive factors. And that such was the case is proved by the fact that no biblical or theological reasoning, no appeal to the community of the faith, ever induced them to change their position.

If I have dealt at some length with this old tradition, it was to show that for Christians to take a position in favor of violence is nothing new at all. From all quarters nowadays we are told that the "theology of revolution" is one of the most remarkable developments in modern theological

thought and that, thanks to it, we shall get rid of the conformism that has long marked the churches. Not so. At most,
this theology represents a return to traditional currents of
thought. I do not disparage it, but I should like to see its partisans moderate their enthusiasm.

I have tried to describe the three positions held by Christians in respect to violence. Formally opposed each to the
others in content, all three are alike in some ways and quite
different in others. The differences, it seems to me, are not so
much a matter of theological disagreement as of temperament. The first position appeals to reasonable (not simply
conformist and hypocritical) Christians who believe that,
after all, every period of human history has its values; that
it is better to try to Christianize a given situation than to
enter into conflict with it; and that one cannot sweep the
whole social and cultural edifice into outer darkness. These
people—they are the prudent ones—practice the virtues of
moderation and temperance. However, the fact is that this
first position, though it is held by many in the Roman church
and in so-called "Christian countries," is much less important today than formerly. While it still has its partisans, they
hardly dare affirm it radically on the doctrinal level.

The second position appeals to those whom I shall call
"sufferers," people who are acutely conscious of the scandal-
ous gap between Christian affirmations and the behavior
of our society. They often feel the sufferings of others so
keenly that they are ready to make serious personal sacrifices. They are marked by true charity, a spirit of sweetness
and, often, great humility. This position was revolutionary
after 1918. It still has many adherents. Yet it is losing ground
today, for two reasons. First, it has been officially recognized
as valid by many churches, hence no longer seems dangerous or extreme. Second, the problems we come up against

today are quite different from those involved in traditional wars and states, and much more difficult to resolve.

The third position appeals to people of passionate temperament, men and women who are uncompromising, hard, incapable of dialogue or moderation. They are obsessed with the question of social justice and the problem of poverty. But for all that they certainly do not exemplify Christian charity. Of course they talk about love. But while the "sufferers" try to practice love of enemy in concrete ways, these people (like the prudent individuals who take the first position) make love a kind of theoretical value. A harsh judgment? It may seem so. But the fact is that these people very easily accept the evil that befalls others. These Christian partisans of violence are not at all inhibited by the thought of the suffering that this violence will inflict on thousands and hundreds of thousands of human beings. No, they have rendered their judgment of what constitutes "justice." The bad people—the powerful, the police, the rich, the communists, the colonializers, the Fascists—deserve to be eliminated. So I cannot call these partisans exemplars of charity in Christ. Their love is selective. They have chosen the "poor." Good enough. But toward the "bad" they are pitiless.

Thus, we see, differences of temperament have an important bearing on those three positions. But, on the other hand, all three are alike in one basic respect. All are what one might call "monist." By that I mean that we are dealing with Christians who think there must be a Christian "solution," a valid way of organizing society or the world. Those who seek a Christian solution try to formulate a compromise between the demands of Christ and the necessities of the world, to work out a quantitative determination, a balance of factors that will bring in a viable social order. Those who seek a plan for reorganizing society on Christian lines make a judgment of society and a demand on the world—the

judgment that the world ought not to be as it is, and the demand that society so change that there will be no more
war, no more poverty, no more exploitation of man; so change
that a Christian finds it satisfactory.

Both these groups, implicitly or explicitly, cherish the
hope that the various elements involved can be brought into
accord. They forget that this is the world that has absolutely rejected Jesus Christ; that there can be no accord between the values, the bases, the *stoikeia* of the world and
those of the revelation.

Certainly, Luther also held a dualistic position—so conceived, however, as to make a separation between the world
and the revealed word. Thus there remained a sort of au-
tonomous sphere for society, to be directed by power,
a power that was completely and directly an expression of
God's action. It seems to me—and I state my view briefly;
I cannot develop it here—that the attempt to assimilate
world and faith to each other is one mistake, and the attempt
to separate them radically is another. It is a mistake to emphasize—as is always done—that the word "world" has several meanings in the Bible, and to suppose that "cosmos"
in the material sense has nothing to do with the world of
power, revolt and opposition that John in particular speaks
of. I think it is society in the first place that is the world of
revolt, rejection and negation.

Again, it is a mistake—an enormous mistake—to suppose
that the Incarnation and Lordship of Jesus Christ have *resolved* the problem. If the Incarnation has a meaning it can
only be that God came into the most abominable of places
(and he did not, by his coming, either validate or change
that place). The "Lordship of Jesus Christ" does not mean
that everything that happens, happens by the decision of
that Lord. No, the world remains the world, but whether
or not it knows it the world is subject to that Lord.

Finally, it is a mistake, and one that is made again and again, to fasten an undue interpretation on the text "God so loved the world," to assume that it implies that the world is not so bad after all. (Incidentally, those who cite the text for this purpose usually omit the rest of it: "so that all may believe"—and that is certainly dishonest.) I believe that the meaning of that passage is precisely the opposite. It is *because* the world is radically, totally evil that nothing less would do than the gift of God's son.

Let us then remember that God's love is utterly boundless, that he loves what is by nature detestable. And let us not say that the world is good, that this word has been given us. So we must stand at a distance from our society, its tendencies and movements, but we must never break with it, for the Incarnation has taken place. We are invited to take part in a dialectic, to be in the world but not of it, and thus to seek out a particular, a specifically Christian position. It is from this point of view that we shall consider this problem of violence, which is so urgent and tragic today.

2

Today's Christians for Violence

IF NOW we proceed to a more detailed consideration of positive, favorable attitudes toward violence, it is (as I said above) because violence seems to be the great temptation in the church and among Christians today. Thirty years ago it was nonviolence, conscientious objection, that constituted the "problem" in the church, and it was this prophetic position that needed to be clarified. Today it is Christians' acceptance of violence, and the theologies thereby engendered, which appear to be the central problem.

Now it seems to me that, in spite of certain World Council of Churches pronouncements on "Church and Society," this problem has been neither clarified nor solved. We must therefore try to describe the situation accurately. Not that this can be expected to bring results, for, as I said above, those who accept violence are scarcely amenable to reason or to factual analysis or to theological arguments. Let us nevertheless proceed.

First a preliminary statement. Very often, it is only after others have brought it into the open that Christians become aware of a problem, and then they climb on the bandwagon of parties or doctrines. That happened in this case, too.

Plunged into a situation of social injustice, exploitation, and alienation, Christians soon discovered movements led by others and enthusiastically joined them. The same thing happened a century ago, when Christians fought in wars for the defense of their country. If I wanted to be mischievous, I would say that a century ago nationalism was the ideological fashion, and Christians went along with it, adducing every imaginable Christian motif to justify their stand. Today social revolution, etc., are the fashion. To say so may seem wicked, for I am told, in scandalized accents, that this is not a question of fashion, that all the truth of Jesus is at stake in this social conflict. But I answer that the Christian nationalists of the nineteenth century also killed each other in the conviction that Jesus had established nations and that love of country was part of love of God. We find that stupid nowadays. But can we be sure that, fifty years hence, today's prorevolutionary position will not also seem stupid?

What troubles me is not that the opinions of Christians change, nor that their opinions are shaped by the problems of the times; on the contrary, that is good. What troubles me is that Christians conform to the trend of the moment without introducing into it *anything* specifically Christian. Their convictions are determined by their social milieu, not by faith in the revelation; they lack the uniqueness which ought to be the expression of that faith. Thus theologies become mechanical exercises that justify the positions adopted, and justify them on grounds that are absolutely not Christian.

Incidentally, it is perhaps pertinent to recall that, in our times, it was in Hitler's Germany that Christian enthusiasm for violence had its start. The *deutsche Christen*—a large majority in the church, at least in the beginning—accepted the chief values set up by the Hitler movement: nation, race, courage, pride, socialism—and violence. Precisely because Hitler accused Christianity of being a religion for the weak and effeminate, for slaves, introverts and cowards, the *deutsche Christen* took up the gauntlet and affirmed that Christianity, too, exalted courage and strength and did not shrink from violence. They declared their readiness to participate in violence in order to attain socially just objectives. The "socially just objectives," of course, were those determined by the Hitler party; and we must not forget that, for the conscientious German of 1933, they were in fact quite as clearly just as the objectives set up by the Communist party are for the communist (and even for a Christian of the extreme left), or as the objectives fixed by the American way of life are for the average American (and for the average Christian American). The acquiescence in violence of the *deutsche Christen* was one of Hitler's victories, the fruits of which we are still reaping. There can be no doubt that it was the Hitler movement that loosed the reign of violence in the world. Concentration camps, racism (and black racism is no more excusable than white racism), torture of enemies, extermination of whole populations—these are used by all regimes today, whether of the right or the left, whether capitalist or socialist. And this is a result of the upheaval that befell the world through Hitler. That violence is so generally condoned today shows that Hitler won his war after all: his enemies imitate him. But, some may protest, everything depends on the objectives; if these are good, we must try to attain them, by whatever means. Here the age-old question of ends and means raises its head again. I shall deal with it later. Now I say only that the act of torturing a human being, though it be intended to advance the noblest of causes, cancels out utterly all intentions and objectives.

That aside. The fact remains that Christians today, far from being repelled by violence, or considering it a possible but shocking necessity, or trying to find a compromise—far from all that—many Christians today participate in "revolutionary" violence just as fervently as, half a century ago, other Christians participated in military violence. And today the hierarchy no longer blesses the major belligerents and their cannon, it blesses the guerrillas. Let us see how that happens.

THE SINGLING OUT OF THE POOR

The singling out, or election, of the poor—this idea is our point of departure. Few themes are more authentically Christian than this one. We moderns have rediscovered that Jesus was the poor man par excellence, that he came for the poor, that it is to the poor that he promised the Kingdom, that the poor man on earth in fact represents Jesus Christ; and we remember that the parable in Matthew 25 (on the judgment of nations) is the central text of the revelation. Theologically, the election of the poor is just.* But unfortunately this theological rediscovery often gives rise to a sentimental attitude toward the poor and merely induces a bad conscience— the sense of being different, of being privileged—in the rich Christian. It is altogether human and normal to be moved by the reality of poverty. But more often than not the result of such emotional reaction is that the poor person is considered a sort of value *an sich*, a sort of embodiment of truth—of truth that takes no account of Jesus Christ. Moreover, these notions are supported by what one might call a prejudice in favor of the collective fostered by socialism.

Here is the first problem for Christians. Is our understanding of the gospel in this regard truly based on faith, on a

* I have developed this theme at length in *L'homme et l'argent* (Neuchâtel and Paris: Delachaux & Niestlé, 1954).

theologically just conception of the poor? Or is it rather shaped by the fact of our living in a world that for a century —ever since the first socialists began the struggle to end poverty—has been listening to socialist ideas? This is by no means merely a formal question, for the outcome of our examination of conscience will depend on where we start from. Now, I say that the rediscovery of the central place of the poor in the gospel was due in great measure to the development of the faith and theological thought. It is solely because they live in a society which views relief of the poor as one of its main concerns that Christians conform to its ideology. Which means that they draw not Christian but sociological consequences.

The first consequence is a generalization: the "poor man" is replaced by "poor people." Instead of being seen in terms of person-to-person relationship and the love of Christ, the problem is posed in global and sociological terms (which proves that the point of departure was humanist and social). The Christian theme of "the poor man" now serves the Christian as a supplementary justification for this collective approach. Thus the whole problem is reduced to one of conflict between the "haves" and the "have-nots," the disinherited peoples. And the conflict can be resolved, not in terms of the love of Christ and his promise (these, of course, are the opium of the people), but in terms of collectivity, economics, institutions. Scores of Christian writings defend this collective approach. Let me quote from one of them—a letter issued by seventeen bishops in September 1967 (a follow-up to the encyclical *Populorum progressio*):

Christians are duty-bound to exhibit true socialism, that is, Christianity integrally lived, with the just division of goods and basic equality. Let us joyfully adopt a form of social life that is better suited to our times and more conformed to the spirit of the gospel. Thus we shall prevent others from confusing God and religion with the oppressors of the poor and the workers. Feudalism, capitalism and imperialism are in fact the oppressors.

The church, with pride and joy, salutes a new humanity, where honor will no longer be accorded to the money accumulated by the few, but to the workers and peasants.

Money has for a long time been cunningly conducting a subversive war throughout the world, has been massacring whole peoples. It is time that the poor peoples, supported and guided by their legitimate governments, were effectively defending their right to life.

If we are to believe these bishops, socialism is the normal expression of Christianity; and it is that precisely because the gospel exalts the poor. For this line of Christian thought directly connects defense of the poor with socialism, and solution of the problem of poverty with socialist government. Once more, both the origin of this view and its socio-economic character are revealed.

But now I must ask American readers to pay strict attention. *I absolutely do not say that capitalism is better than socialism.* I firmly believe the contrary. *I absolutely do not say that defense of the poor through socialist movements is wrong.* I firmly believe the contrary. I want only to show what a mistake it is to confuse Christianity and socialism; they are not the same thing. A while ago, people made the monumental error of saying that democracy, liberalism, competitive capitalism were all expressions of Christianity. Today they make the same monumental error for the benefit of socialism.

But to assimilate poverty and socialism, and socialism and Christianity, is to introduce the theme of violence (as the pastoral letter quoted above shows clearly). For it is only by violence that the defense of the poor can really be assured—there have been enough kind words, promises and so on. Only violence is effectual in the face of exploitation, coercion and oppression by the rich and their governments. As Karl Kautsky said, in criticism of Eduard Bernstein: "Why, in a world of violence, should only the proletariat not have the right to use violence?" A highly valid argument coming from a socialist; but today it is gospel truth for a great many Christians, indeed *for the best* and most serious Christians—those who think of Christianity as something more than words and kind sentiments. I share their deep concern, their revolutionary will. But for that very reason I am the more distressed to see them mistake the way. To them it seems obvious that when the forces of imperialism and colonialism contend violently against the peoples who are now assimilated to the poor of the gospel, those forces can be countered only by violence; it is only through fighting that man will win freedom. Therefore, and quite understandably, they reject the familiar themes of Christianity. One writer states their case as follows:

The gospel's sweetness, for example, is suspect; it looks too much like its caricatures: irresolution and readiness to compromise—often profitably—with the established disorders; the kind of popularity that easily camouflages betrayal; a certain interior, narcissistic complacency—the secret self-vindication of the ineffectual weakling. Such deviations are very real, and they are so frequently exemplified among Christians that the word "sweet" evokes these images. . . . Moreover, many nowadays are irritated by the supernatural character of the gospel's sweetness. Man no longer thinks he needs grace in order to obtain what he considers natural.*

To this I shall add that, in the eyes of many people, love of the poor seems better expressed and incarnated by socialists than by Christians.

But we must also take note of a painfully obvious limi-

* Régamey, *op. cit.*, pp. 172–174 (French edition).

tation in this regard. Christian love is addressed to a man, to a neighbor or several neighbors; it is an interindividual matter. But what should, what can it do about the misery that results from an economic system, a form of social organization? In such a case Christianity seems ineffectual. It can deal with the consequences of injustice but cannot act against the bases of injustice; it is concerned for the misery of some individuals but does not see the multitude of the poor. It even plays the role of what Paul Nizan calls "watchdog"; that is, to the extent that it calms passions or preaches patience or permits the poor man to bear his poverty or holds up the light of hope, to that extent it becomes a party to injustice, inhibits revolt against it and supports evil. We certainly must take cognizance of this important fact.

Before the nineteenth century, poverty was generally thought of as a destiny, a fate, one of the great scourges of mankind, along with famine, wild beasts, epidemics, war, earthquakes. These were natural disasters. One could only accept them, be patient and live in hope; and mutual love was a great help and solace in times of trial (in *La Peste*, Camus shows that it still is). But for a century now people have realized that poverty is not a fate, not of the same nature as cyclones, but the result of forms of social and economic organization. Therefore, merely (*merely!*) changing that organization will end poverty. But anything that tends to perpetuate poverty or to divert forces that should be devoted to this collective struggle, is treason to the poor. And that is why Christians are trying to work out a "Christian social ethic"—trying to show, for example, that love is addressed not to a neighbor but to collectivities, etc. These Christians want to "put Christianity back on course," and since, nowadays, championing the poor implies violence, they accept violence; because, they say, the love the gospel speaks of is utterly useless in this world of ours. Moreover, they insist that in a world divided between oppressed and oppressors, between poor and powerful, we must take sides. It is impossible to deny that this division exists, or to point out that there is also a third force at work, or to evade the issue in some other way; for, we are told (and on the whole rightly), such evasion amounts to condoning oppression, therefore siding with the oppressor. This indeed seems indisputable. Every time I remain silent or passive in the face of evil, I reinforce evil. Therefore the Christian *must* side with the oppressed. And there is only one way of doing that; namely, violence, since it is by violence that they are oppressed. Nonviolence is sheer betrayal; it gives free rein to the violence visited upon others. Nonviolence is indeed "super-violence" (as it has been called), because the man who in effect acquiesces in the oppression of the poor by violence, is convinced that he is thus keeping his heart pure and his hands clean. So the proponent of nonviolence not only is good for nothing; he is contemptible. So goes the first line of argument that leads Christians to accept the idea of violence and to associate themselves with violent movements.

THE BASIC PRESUPPOSITIONS

But acceptance of violence rests also on certain presuppositions—shared by both Christians and non-Christians —which we must clarify, for they are the "key ideas" in our problem. These presuppositions are what might be called ready-made ideas, completely irrational ideas that linger in the unconscious like an ideology and are unquestioningly accepted as facts.

The first presupposition is that material want is the most important of all problems. Yet for centuries man has tried to show that there are other elements in human life that are more important than material poverty; that to demand comfort, material goods at any price is a serious error. It was with the Industrial Revolution, as society plunged ever more eagerly into the conquest of material riches and bent all its energies to the accumulation of goods, that material poverty became a major problem. Obviously, this meant abandonment or downgrading of spiritual values, virtue, etc. To share or not to share in the increase of the collective wealth —this was the Number One question. It was the desire to acquire wealth that prompted the poor to start fighting. And the rich were hypocrites when they accused the poor (who were no longer interested in "spiritual values") of materialism. For the rich had given the example and set society on the acquisitive path. The great business of the whole society, and therefore of all its members, was to increase consumption of goods. But obviously, the moment this is the first objective, the ideal, lack of goods is the principal drama.

Historically, it is not true that man was obsessed from the beginning by the need of eating and being comfortable. These were of course important, but they were not the key to his behavior. The concern for material goods became paramount when "civilization"—particularly our civilization—had reached a certain level. The King of the Two Sicilies put the matter concretely when he said to the King of Piedmont (this was in the nineteenth century): "It is plain that the people of Turin have many more things than the people of Palermo. . . . But in my country the people are happy, in yours they are sad." The passionate concern to consume the requisite number of calories and to possess goods in abundance is a modern phenomenon. Let no one say that it was perhaps because of their ignorance or apathy or stupidity that people did not conceive of life in those terms. Let no one say that it was because they had no other choice and that they compensated for their material poverty by "sublimations." No; they had a different conception, a different ideal of life. But again I warn the reader against drawing a false conclusion. "So the poor man is happier!" *I never said that.* It all depends on your idea of happiness. Dancing, fighting, experiencing religious ecstasy, working, eating a steak or owning an automobile—whatever your idea, you will find happiness in realizing it. But —for a thousand reasons I cannot go into here—it is society that expresses, constructs and proposes conceptions of happiness; and the members of the society participate in them.

Thus in a society like ours it would never be suggested that the poor should be persuaded to seek happiness elsewhere than in the consumption of goods. Every inequality of consumption is felt to be a frightful injustice, because consumption is the Number One objective of the social body. Regrettable, perhaps, but we must take things as they are. And Christians, too, accept that objective. But when society puts the practice of virtue in second place and in fact downgrades spiritual values (even if it still proclaims them officially), when the ideal of man is no longer of a moral or religious type, the inevitable consequence of all these mistakes is another mistake: violence. There is a correlation here. *To the ideal of high consumption and the downgrading of spiritual values corresponds a conception of injustice that centers exclusively on the problem of consumption; and equality in consumption cannot be achieved except by violence.* That this is so seems the more evident in view of a belief widely held today, even among Christians; namely, that no man is worthy of that name unless he is fairly well off financially and enjoys a certain level of consumption. All of us to some degree share the conviction that spiritual life

develops out of, and in step with, material life.* A Christian
wrote several years ago: "Preaching the gospel to hungry
people is useless. What we should send to Africa and India
is not missionaries, but food and engineers." First, feed them,
take care of their material needs, put an end to their misery;
then we'll see about preaching.

But this raises a question. It is a fact that in the time of
the prophets and even in the time of Jesus, Israel was terribly poor. Its condition was very much like that described
in the words, "Two-thirds of humanity is dying of hunger."
Well, did the prophets and Jesus proclaim that they would
not deliver the revelation until Israel's economic problem
was solved? However, let us not use that to excuse the rich
who refuse to help the poor—but are certainly ready to send
them spiritual aid. Rather, let us say that if an earnest Christian can write what the one quoted above did, it is solely
because he shares the common presupposition of our times:
that poverty is the great calamity and therefore an obstacle to the spiritual life; that the real problem is how to induce the rich to aid the poor; and that otherwise preaching
the gospel is hypocrisy. In other words, the sole serious problem is the unequal division of material goods.

Let me say one thing more in regard to this presupposition, this idea that everybody accepts. It might seem strange
that people can simultaneously hold both the ideas mentioned above; namely, that the poor man represents Jesus
Christ on earth, and therefore all the right is on his side,
and he is the only one who must be considered; but at the
same time, that poverty is a scandal, and we must do our
best to get rid of this scandal and to put the poor into a "nor-

* I cannot analyze this idea here. I have already done so at length in
two books: *Exégèse des nouveaux lieux communs* (Paris, 1966) and *Mét-
amorphose du bourgeois* (Paris, 1967).

mal" situation; that is, put an end to poverty. Contradictory as these two ideas seem, Christians usually entertain both together.

Moreover (as they have been from time to time in the past), Christians today are once more convinced that justice is the preeminent value, the value that transcends all others. But they conceive of justice in the sense of equality, in a social sense, as requiring more equitable division of consumers' goods. And this makes violence necessary. But from another point of view this conception of justice is a reaction against the pangs of conscience that trouble most Christians. They are well aware that today's church is made up of rich people and intellectuals and socially prominent personages, that it is a pillar of society. And this awareness quite naturally provokes a crisis of conscience in Christians; for the church is not what it ought to be, and the church supports an unjust society.

Then, too, Christians are convinced that the church can no longer play its traditional role in regard to the poor—the role of assistance, partial response, individual aid, palliative measures—because, as they see it, the problem is no longer that of the poor individual but of the system; and to ameliorate the situation of some poor people is in fact to reinforce the system, and to end injustice for one individual is to refrain from combating social injustice.

Now all these factors together lead to the conclusion that violence is necessary and that Christians should participate in it. Thus they are carried away by a whole complex of emotions and ideas: authentic spirituality, aspiration for a true church, suffering with the poorest of the poor; but also: sociological conformism, assent to commonplace notions, a bad social conscience (which relieves the individual of his responsibility), extremist and excessive simplification (for it must never be forgotten that recourse to violence is always

and above all an act of inhuman simplification). Alexander
cut the Gordian knot, yes. But he was totally a soldier.

The second presupposition on which Christian acceptance of violence is based can be summarized in the now
commonplace formula, "Man has come of age"—a formula
expressing the Christian point of view of its author, Dietrich
Bonhoeffer. It means that up to now in his history, man was
somehow kept in the bondage of childhood by the powers
that be, the state, etc., and by the idea of a "father-God,"
so that he did not dare to affirm himself fully. Now, thanks
to his technology, man has acquired power, has got rid of
his guardians and of the idea of God's fatherhood, and at
the same time has acquired a new, a rational and scientific
mentality. No longer does he credit all the old religious
stories, no longer does he believe in the existence of a num-
inous something, etc. He can assert himself: "I count; nothing else does." Let me point out that this attitude—contrary
to those who consider it a great new thing in human history
—does not seem to be at all new. It is the very old attitude,
described at length in the Bible, of human pride, which has
always tried to break away from God; it is the "will to power."
What is really new is that, instead of realizing that all this
is the manifestation of an ancient evil (*potestatis cupido,
avitum malum!*) and of the lost condition of man, who seeks
a way out of his complex of "despairing power"—what is
really new is that Christians today find this prideful attitude
excellent and consonant with the dignity of man. By breaking loose from God's ancient tutelage, they believe, man
has graduated into an authentic situation. As a matter of
fact, there is a whole theological school which holds that
man's unaided self-realization is the ideal to be striven after.
    There is only one explanation of this "conversion" of
Christians to the spirit of power; namely, conformism to

today's technological society and awe at the advances of science. Obviously, such conformism entails a series of results. In the first place, it entails rejection of the ethical consequences of man's condition as a sinner in need of forgiveness. Man-come-of-age does not need to practice humility and resignation; he can and must affirm his domination (and the Genesis texts commanding man to dominate the world are actually cited in support of this view). He must have no inhibitions about using the means of power that are at his disposal, must not let humility deter him from acting. Nor must he be resigned, since modern technology generally permits him to master his problems, and in any case no problem is irremediable. So the virtues of humility and resignation are rejected as despicable, and every effort is made to show that they have nothing to do with Christianity —in spite of all the biblical passages to the contrary. Indeed (as usual) sociological arguments are advanced to counter these passages: it was the hypocritical bourgeois who, taking a cue from Machiavelli, preached humility and resignation (and also poverty), in order to persuade the exploited and alienated masses to accept their condition; therefore these "virtues" must be rejected. Strange reasoning! But you come across it again and again. It is, of course, quite true that the bourgeoisie and the rich have used (or misused) the gospel to assure their own dominance. Well, what then? Is the truth less the truth because the liar mouths it? When Satan set Jesus on the pinnacle of the temple and said: "Throw yourself down; for it is written, He will give his angels charge of you"—did the word of God cease to be the word of *God* because Satan cited it? Should forgiven man cease being humble because the bourgeoisie has exploited humility? To accuse the rich of hypocrisy is certainly justified. But to tell the Christian, "Stop being humble, because you have come of age through technology," seems to me monstrous. And as to the comfort the gospel speaks of, it seems that Christianity ought no longer to be the comforter of the poor and the afflicted, because, forsooth, "if you comfort them you divert them from seeking material, concrete means for ending their misery; if they are comforted by faith, they will not set to work to solve the economic problems."

And Jesus' saying about "the one thing necessary"—that, of course, is also rejected as the product of a prescientific mentality. Here, too, the charge of hypocrisy is raised: to comfort a man by the gospel and the ideal of the kingdom is a maneuver intended to dissuade him from claiming the material goods that are his due. This notion begets a new idea of proper behavior. Many theologians think that it is unworthy of man to plead for the goods he needs, to pray, to take the posture of a suppliant or a beggar (though the Beatitudes bid us do just that). Man's dignity demands that he be the proud master of things and seize what he needs by conquest.

Now, sadly enough, it is a fact that Christians have humiliated the poor. But again, does the wrongful attitude of the possessors affect the truth? It seems to me that in passage after passage the Bible condemns man's pretentious notion that his own powers are sufficient to achieve justice and secure his rights. But this means little to our theologians. The politico-economic reality is the only one that counts, and it is clear that in this field man must be a conqueror. So paternalism is rejected *in toto*. The rich and powerful who try to find a valid solution for poverty and to improve the condition of the poor are either showing their contempt of the poor or fooling them. Who will admit that the colonizer prepares the colonized for independence, that the proprietor provides social services for his workers, or even that the teacher maintains a guardian authority over his students? Every such "guardianship" is viewed as a criminal attack on the dignity of the "inferiors." Nor does the church escape censure. Its role as mother of the faithful—the mother who tends and supports and aids them—is passé. Man-come-of-age no longer needs such "mothering": he will do everything himself.

It is easy to see at what point these two propositions— uncritically accepted as they are—tend toward the development of a climate of violence. Humility, resignation, the gospel's comfort, prayer are all useless. Violence will take care of everything. The protest against paternalism and against the church's mother-role means that man does not want to receive anything from a superior; he wants to take it himself. The benefit given by a superior is worth much less than the same benefit wrested from a vanquished superior. That is why, in today's political and social conflicts, the concessions made by a superior never avail; for people do not want concessions, they want to grab something from the superior. The moment he yields, his concession ceases to be of interest. It is exactly this kind of thing that many Christians defend nowadays. In their eyes it demands and justifies violence.

THE THREE POSSIBLE ORIENTATIONS

Christians who approve of violence do so out of one of three very different conceptions of Christianity. For one group, Christianity is a revolutionary force; for a second group, there is a theology of revolution (man-made); for a third, Christianity has been fused into the revolution, which has become a value in itself. Let us examine these three conceptions.

As a matter of fact, the first does not really imply violence. It is based on the idea, central to Christianity, of the coming Kingdom of God and the second coming of Jesus Christ, and it involves an interpretation of what God requires of man. Time was when the will of God was understood as a point of departure; now, it is understood rather as a summons, a call. In the first instance, the Law, affirmed as the fixed and immutable expression of God's eternal will, and spelled out in theological and ethical formulas, was the sole and sufficient guide for man's conduct. The ideal of human conduct constructed on the basis of this concept of God's will was necessarily moralistic and—the important point for our purposes—static; change was out of the question. The truth was given, and everything had to be "deduced" from Christian principles.

This interpretation has of course been widely criticized and largely abandoned. Today, living the Christian life is thought of as a being-at-work in history—not past but future history; as a creative tension toward the future, the history that is still to be traversed. No longer is history the unrolling of an already painted curtain. And it is this eschatological tension that gives the Christian presence in the world its revolutionary vigor.* Several factors account for this vigor. On the one hand there is the coming kingdom; but because he is coming, the Lord is already among us here and now, and we must act here and now, in this society, because God's kingdom, God's new creation, is near. Therefore we cannot be content with this society. We must examine everything, question everything, in the light of the kingdom. We may never stop and say, "Now justice is established, now we have set up a valid society in which we

---

* This is a summary of a number of long articles I wrote on this subject. I believe I was one of the first to maintain that Christianity is revolutionary. Cf. "Christianisme et révolution," *Le semeur,* 1936; "Le Christianisme puissance révolutionnaire," in *Présence au monde moderne,* 1948, English edition, *The Presence of the Kingdom* (New York: Seabury, 1967; paperback).

can peaceably await the coming of the Lord." Every advance realized in church and society must immediately be ana- lyzed, criticized, measured by the kingdom yardstick. The kingdom demands nothing less than radical change. Mind, in all this, we certainly must not get the idea that we are "preparing" the kingdom, that it is brought nearer by every progressive step we take socially, economically, politically, etc., and that in the end we build it; as if *we* with our ideas could build the kingdom! The kingdom is a revolutionary magnitude that cannot be measured by our measuring sticks; and, being immeasurable, it reveals the vanity of what is. Such is the first source of Christianity's revolutionary vigor.

But, on the other hand, the coming kingdom of God is also the kingdom of heaven that is already present, hidden in the world (the treasure, the yeast, the seed), working in the world and changing it mysteriously. This gives rise to a sec- ond orientation: the Christian should be on the lookout, vigilant to discern signs of that working, ready to become himself a sign of that hidden life. This is not the attitude of a man who, on his own responsibility, demands change be- cause he expects the kingdom to break in. It is an attitude of submission, patience, openness, in the confidence that God is at work in the present; an attitude that determines how the Christian should act with reference both to the future (which is given by God) and to the hidden present (where God reveals himself). That is why, in relation to future and present, the Christian is qualified to be ambassador, sen- tinel or sacrificer. And indeed he sometimes plays these roles when he intervenes in the affairs of the world. However, the Christian's action must be specifically Christian. Chris- tians must never identify themselves with this or that poli- tical or economic movement. Rather, they must bring to

social movements what they alone can provide. Only so can
they signalize the kingdom. So far as they act like the others
—even to forward social justice, equality, etc.—I say that
there is no sense and nothing specifically Christian in acting like the others.* In fact, the political and revolutionary
attitude proper to the Christian is radically different from
the attitude of others; it is specifically Christian, or else it
is nothing.

But here let me emphasize that, while it *may* bear upon
other (i.e., not specifically Christian) objects, have other
parameters, use other methods, this Christian revolutionary
attitude does not necessarily correspond (though it may
do so) to what is called revolution in society. And let me
emphasize especially that this Christian attitude by no
means implies violence. Indeed the revolution that the Christian is called to carry always in his heart and to weave into
the fabric of daily life and of the life of society, must not take
the form of violence. I ask only this: Let us apply the two
commandments absolutely; let us apply them without so-
phistical attempts to weaken their binding power, without
taking account of the established values, orders, salaries,
classes—and then we shall see the whole society fall to
pieces, without violence. (I shall return to this matter later
on.)

The main thing is that we entertain no delusions as to our

---

* Of course, there will be objections: "But we want to be people like and
with the others in our society. We don't want Christianity to separate us
from our fellow men." I know this story, and I should like things to be that
way. But then I ask you to be serious—to stop talking about Christianity
and pretending to be a Christian when you act like that. Then let go of
everything that differentiates you from the others—particularly the faith
and the name of Jesus Christ. But mind, if you do that you will be separating
yourself from those who refuse to conform, those who still confess Jesus
Christ as their Lord and Savior.

capacity to accomplish this. Let us acknowledge that if Christian action must be specifically Christian, it can be so only if it represents radical application of the word of God; otherwise, Christianity is not revolutionary, and then the door is opened to all the violent and revolutionizing heresies we shall presently discuss. But let us keep in mind that if these heresies are rife—as they are—the fault lies with those who call themselves Christians but keep for their own the treasure the Lord has entrusted to them.

We come now to the theologians of revolution. Their approach is something like this: Since there *are* revolutions in the world, and since, from a human point of view, they may seem to be legitimate, is it not possible to develop a theology of these revolutions and to discover a relation between them and Christianity? For Christianity must not remain forever linked with the established powers. This reasoning takes no account of the fact that the Christian revolutionary spirit is specific. Rather (and I say this a bit maliciously) its proponents are concerned to get Christianity "out of customs"—to persuade secular revolutionists that Christianity has rid itself of its old conformisms and its rapport with the state, capitalism, colonialism, etc. It seems to me useful to emphasize that this concern finds support in the work of exegetes who try to make out that Jesus was an advocate of violence, a revolutionary in the current sense. A number of studies have been published which identify Jesus with the Zealots and explain the crucifixion as a political act. Mr. Cullmann has disposed of these in a thoroughly convincing manner.* (Nevertheless, these ideas have been taken up again of late from a non-Christian point of view.) Mr. Car-

* Oscar Cullmann, *Dieu et César* (Neuchâtel and Paris: Delachaux & Niestlé, 1956).

michael * declares that the important moment in the life
of Jesus came with his "seizure and occupation of the temple in Jerusalem . . . the essential point is that Jesus drives
out the priests, the merchants, and holds the Roman gar-
rison [*Roman* indeed!] in check. And the central word of
Jesus would be, 'I come not to bring peace but a sword.'
Moreover, the gospel attests that his disciples were
armed. . . . Jesus is the head of an organized movement
against Rome and against those Jews who are traitors to their
country." Carmichael attempts to show that the "true" meaning of Jesus' life lies in his consecration of recourse to violent
insurrection for the triumph of justice on earth and in the
"beyond." But this study has hardly been referred to by
the people who are in search of a theology of revolution,
and indeed its exegesis is so feeble, so forced, that they cannot but view it askance and construct their system on the
basis of other principles and theological arguments.

The quest of a theology of revolution is pursued in Catholic as well as Protestant circles. Among studies in this field
made by Catholics, let me cite those of Father Peuchmaurd,
who considers himself as in the lineage of classical
theology.† For example, he declares that St. Thomas's assertion that the poor man was justified in stealing must now
be more widely applied to classes and nations: "The pro-
letarian nations have a claim on the goods of the rich nation
next door." And he draws a parallel between passages in the
encyclical *Populorum progressio* and some of Fidel Castro's

---

* Joel Carmichael, "L'Épée de Jesus," *Nouvelle revue française*, 1966. The
same ideas are advanced in the U.S.A. Pastor Albert Cleage writes: "Jesus
was the colored leader of a colored people carrying on a national struggle
against a white people. . . . The activities of Jesus must be understood
from this point of view: a man's effort to lead his people from oppression to
freedom" (i.e., political freedom). *Le Monde*, January, 1968.

† Peuchmaurd: *Parole et mission*, 1967.

statements. The pope indicated that an insurrection cannot be condemned if the evils resulting from it are less grave than the evils it seeks to remedy (the same test as for a just war). Castro says the same thing: "Not the revolutionary struggle but the misery caused by exploitation costs the most lives." Therefore, Father Peuchmaurd says, "one cannot a priori exclude the participation of Christians in the revolution on the ground that it involves violence; we are called to restore prophetism—not a verbal but a responsible prophetism"—that is, a revolutionary prophetism. But what a misinterpretation of the term prophetism! Prophet of what and of whom? And just what biblical prophets substituted revolutionary activity for proclamation of the judgment of God? Enough on that score. Yet Father Peuchmaurd is not as bold as some Protestant theologians, for he points out that revolutionary violence is not a value in itself: "The Christian will carry the call for Reconciliation to the very heart of Revolution."

However, among French Catholics, Father Cardonnel is the most representative of the theologians of revolution.* He asserts emphatically: "The gospel (without in the least slighting any other of the things it preaches) must be interpreted as requiring abolition of the class system, an end of the American bombing of Vietnam and of the wasteful armaments competition, and the obliteration of anachronistic frontiers." In support of his views he naturally adduces the words of the prophets, who—obviously, in his opinion—preached "social justice." (More careful analysis of these passages reveals that they call for something altogether different and lead in an altogether different direction!) Father Cardonnel adds: "God is not the dominator, but the awakener of guerrillas among oppressed peoples. Unless we

* Conference on the Gospel and Revolution, March 22, 1968.

participate in the struggle of the poor for their liberation, we can understand nothing about Jesus Christ. . . . How shall we observe Lent nowadays? By making, each of us, a revolutionary rupture with a society based on injustice, and by paralyzing the death mechanisms of the money system —if necessary, by a well-planned general strike. Such is the Lent that pleases God, the Easter liturgy of today." Plainly, there are remarkable confusions in these proposals. To say that a strike is the liturgy God desires is a fine bit of oratory, but it does not really mean anything. And indeed I am bound to say that all these ideas imply an astonishing ignorance of political and sociological phenomena. As to prophetism, every visionary sect, from Montanism on, has pretended to be prophetic—a case of confusing prophetism with verbal delirium!

Protestant studies on the theology of revolution are becoming very numerous.* Let me summarize succinctly their general line of argument. In the first place, these theologians are on the whole convinced that God is at work in the revolutionary movement of modern times. (This is the inverse of the old position, which saw historical events as acts of God: *gesta Dei per Francorum!*) On the other hand, they admit that the world of power and injustice is the expression of sin; and indeed it is "in the heart of revolutionary negation of that sinful reality that God's 'No' becomes audible in the social domain." Here, too, we have simply the inverse of the traditional position: that it was the government which was

* As examples I cite Richard Shaull, "Revolutionary Change in Theological Perspective," and H. D. Wendlend, "The Theology of the Responsible Society," in *Christian Social Ethics in a Changing World,* John C. Bennett, ed. (New York: Association Press, and London: SCM Press, 1966); Arthur Rich, "La révolution, problème théologique," Borosov, "Rôle de la théologie dans les révolutions sociales," and Richard Shaull, "Le défi révolutionnaire lancé a la théologie," in the journal *Christianisme social* (Nos. 1 and 2; Paris, 1967).

charged to put down the overflowing of sin, and that the order established by the state was the expression of God's "No" to disorder, violence, etc. But again: "In a world that has become revolution-minded the believer is commissioned to live as a revolutionary and to do his part in assuring change." Once more, it is the world that dictates how the Christian shall act; since he lives in the midst of a society where revolutionary movements are rife, he must take his cue from that society. And he must bear witness that "the essence of revolution is indeed the irruption of God's sovereignty in the world." This statement inverses what I said above in speaking of Christianity as a revolutionary power. But what is perhaps most characteristic of this whole attempt to formulate a theology of revolution is that its proponents seem unable to put their "theology" on a firm basis. So what they give us is a scattering of theses, none of which is profound or far-reaching. One of these theologians declares that the key is to be found in the word of Jesus (John 14:12):* "He who believes in me will also do the works that I do; and greater works than these will he do . . ."—these "greater works" being the struggle against hunger, misery, sickness, social injustice; that is, revolution. Another attempts to assimilate the Christian with the revolutionary vocabulary: "Revolution restores the relation of man to man; it is a transformation of life, a renewal, a regeneration, a new life" —in other words, the equivalent of conversion. "The essential thing in the revolution is radical renewal, new life, liberty for the future"—and these are also the work of faith. Again: "The Christian life begins in crisis and continues in a state of crisis"—but what is this *Krisis?* Revolution, of course! Others of these theologians undertake to show that the events the Bible describes as concerning individuals

---

* Josef Smolik, *Christianisme social,* 1967.

and revealing God's relation to man on the personal level—
that these events must be transcribed into sociological and
collective terms: "Repentance—this radical break with the
former way of life, this engagement of one's whole being in
a new life, applies not only to the individual but to the whole
of society, nation, class. . . . Repentance is a call to revolution!" The procedure is plain to see: translation of the personal into the collective, capped by an absolutization of
terms; for example, "conversion," not to Jesus Christ but "in
oneself"; "repentance," no longer repentance in the Nine-
veh sense of turning to the true God, but a social act, an act
"in itself," having no relation to the word of God. So, by sup-
pressing all reference to God and God's word, Christian beliefs can easily be interpreted as consonant with revolution.
Half a century ago, there was a similar development in regard to faith, which was then viewed as a value "in itself,"
a psychic, psychological value. Apparently no one perceived
that in the gospel it was not faith that counted but He in
whom one had faith. Today the same little surgical operation is performed in the name of revolution.

True, some of these theologians, speaking from another
point of view, declare that "Christians must bring Christian
social fervor to the social revolutions of our time." Another
expression of the pervasive notion that the function of
Christians is to supplement what other people do. The chief
proponent of this line of thought, in addition to Arthur Rich,
is Richard Shaull. The most important fact of our times,
Shaull asserts, is the revolutionary fact. The confrontation of
groups, races, classes that is going on all over the world indicates that the social revolution is the principal problem;
for, in Shaull's opinion, our society is extremely malleable,
and technology opens up possibilities of "justice and well-
being" for all. The social structures are less and less stable
because they are losing their sacred character; hence the

eruption of messianic movements that propose to free man
from all that enslaves and dehumanizes him. This being the
situation, Shaull believes that "revolution is our fate," that
therefore we must devise new political and social categories.
Moreover, this revolutionary situation is "a challenge to the
church." "If we want to preserve the most precious values of
our cultural and religious heritage, we cannot stay out of the
revolutionary struggle. There is no other responsible attitude,
whatever the issue."

Let me point out first that, as a piece of sociological analysis, the above is sadly wanting. Rather than conveying to the
reader a just conception of a technological society, it rouses
his emotions, confuses him as to the difference between socialism and revolution, and betrays him into mere sentimentality about inequality and wealth. Well, it seems to me that
basing an ethic and a new theological departure on factual
errors is a serious matter. Even if it were to be granted that
the Christian ethic must be adapted to a sociological context, the sociological analysis must still be sound; approxima-
tions and generalizations will not do. This is the more important because Shaull insists that the Christian must participate in the revolution (since in his eyes the revolution is
the Fact), whatever the consequences—a palpable *non se-
quitur*, it seems to me, for to say that the Christian must
participate is to make revolution a value, even in a sense an
absolute value! In any case, when Shaull resumes a theological point of view he rediscovers in a theology the theses mentioned above: Christianity is revolutionary, it deconsecrates,
it orients us toward a future that is always to be created,
messianism must not be forgotten on earth, and the kingdom
of God is a dynamic reality which judges the social order.
All this is true, and I shall not deal with it again.

But here, too, Shaull indicates that the revolutions going
on in the world are the controlling factor. Instead of arriv-

ing at a specific revolutionary orientation on the basis of theological reflection, he confuses the revolutionary tension of
messianism with the social revolutions, however extreme,*
which break out for a thousand reasons.

To sum up Shaull's position: since the Christian faith has
a revolutionary content, the Christian should participate in
all revolutions without reference to Christianity. Obviously,
revolution is the overriding value, therefore the main argument; to be a revolutionary is more important than to be, or
not to be, a Christian. Of course, Shaull will object vehe-
mently to this summing up of his position and will protest
that he never wrote anything of the sort; but in fact these
propositions underlie his whole proposal. Moreover, looking
again to his theological bases, he discovers there the idea of
the humanization of society. He is convinced, on the one
hand, that the work of God in Christ is a work of humanization; and, on the other, that the objective of revolutions is
humanization. Thus revolution is inserted into the category
of the humanizing activity of God. And, almost inevitably,
the conclusion follows that it is God himself who is demolishing the old structures in order to create a more human existence. In other words, God is at the center of the struggle
led by the revolutionaries; such is the essence of revolution!

Naturally, theologians like Shaull do not consider whether
what they call the "humanizing" work of God is the same
thing as what revolutions aim at. To be sure, there is Vladi-
mir Mayakovsky's poem, but that does not seem to me a
quite sufficient argument. Again, these theologians do not
consider even for a second that forces other than God might
be at work, that, very likely, the Prince of this world also has

---

* I am well aware that "extreme" is not altogether accurate, for Shaull
would reject a Nazi revolution with horror. Yet this was a revolution as important, as profound, as radical, etc., as any of today's movements—and as
revolutionary.

a finger in revolutions. Finally, they make no distinctions among revolutions; communist, nationalist, justificatory, tribal, Francoist revolutions—they approve them all, though they accord Marxism a privileged position. But it must be recognized that Shaull does now and then make reservations as to the results of revolution. He realizes that the revolutionary is tempted to believe that he can, alone and unaided, solve all problems and create a new order, while the Christian knows (or ought to know) that political strife can bring only limited results. But these are insignificant reservations, and Shaull cancels them by declaring that "the new order established by the revolution is a gift."

So revolution must be accepted. But the Christian who accepts it finds himself paralyzed on two fronts. The most serious lacuna in Shaull's thought is his failure to deal with the means of revolution. I have tried elsewhere to show that the question of means is central in the search for a present-day Christian ethic. Shaull does not say a word about means. And that is why, though he is the most important of the theologians of revolution, he is not important for our purposes. He does not seem to think that violence is the chief means of revolution—though if this is indeed his view it raises problems for Christians. He only imagines, somewhat idealistically, that it might be possible to create a political guerrilla force through organizing small revolutionary cells. And he says that the church, if it is prepared to take its vocation seriously, "must constitute the frame in which men will be made available for that revolutionary encounter."

As to violence itself, Shaull rejects Wendlend's dictum that Christians may participate only in nonviolent action. Instead, Shaull offers an admirable formula: "There can be situations in which the use of violence alone can set the process of transformation in motion. What is important is not to know whether violence is required, but to know whether the use of violence, when it is absolutely necessary, is oriented toward a strategy of continuing struggle for limited changes, or whether its objective is the total destruction of the social order." Certainly there is no better way of evading the problem of violent means. Yet in Shaull's theological perspective, this problem would be basic; in fact he asks: "What are the specific elements of God's humanizing activity in the world?" And he answers: forgiveness, freedom, justice, reconciliation. Revolutionary structures, he adds, cannot serve this design except by providing occasion for *each social group* to participate more fully in shaping the community's economic and national life. Apparently it does not occur to him that the means of revolution are the exact opposite of forgiveness, justice, etc., and that revolutions generally propose the elimination of social groups by violence. Thus Shaull not only is silent on the problem of means; he has no clear idea of what a Christian ethic could contribute to a definition of ends. He takes refuge in a situational ethic—an ethic that condones any objective society decides on. I can only say that this doctrine is idealistic, theologically negligible, and all but totally unrealistic.

Finally, the third orientation toward violence. This is exemplified by a small group of French Franciscans and their publication, *Frères du Monde*. (I do not know whether there are similar groups in countries other than France, though I would not be surprised if there are.) These Franciscans are at the extreme limit of Christian revolutionary thought. In fact Father Maillard, the director of *Frères du Monde*, actually declared: "If I noticed that my faith [true, he did not add "Christian"] separated me by however little from other men and diminished my revolutionary violence, I would not hesitate to sacrifice my faith." A clear statement of the conviction latent in Shaull's writings; namely, that revolution is more fundamental than the faith. But does Father Maillard really believe that one must choose between the Christian faith and revolutionary violence? I think not. I think rather that what he is saying is this: Revolutionary violence is to such a degree the only possible expression of the Christian faith that, if I suspect that my faith is leading me to become less violent, I am mistaken about the content of the faith and must abandon it; because, having decided for violence, I am sure that I am in the true Christian succession.

Let me point out here that Father Maillard shares the motivations common to all these "revolutionary" Christians; concern for the poor, solidarity with the Third World, dissatisfaction with capitalist injustice, etc. Indeed he says that "to love the Third World is to love *its* revolution and to side with it, to be in it, in the hope of being able to remain there as a nonviolent participant, without judging those who, though they kill others, give their own life too." Here Father Maillard describes himself as nonviolent. Elsewhere, however, he writes: "Violence is imposed on us from outside: I must confront it. To refuse to take a gun is to stand by while injustice does its work and the poor die of hunger. It is always the violence of the oppressor that prompts the counterviolence of the oppressed; matters reach a pass where the poor can cope with the situation only by violence."

But he does not merely state the fact: he justifies it. And this leads him to astonishing conclusions. "We must free ourselves from a morality of purity." In other words, he poses the problem of means, but does not hesitate to condone the worst means: "We must respect every man *who decides to participate.*" No longer is it the neighbor who is important, but participation. And as to solidarity with others, the main thing, certainly, is not the community of faith but revolutionary action. "The Christian as such does not interest me. I care only about the man who shows his concern for his brothers on a global level. If he truly wants to save mankind, we shall solve the problem of means together." What then is the meaning of the Communion of Saints? In Father Maillard's theology, it is the revolutionaries—not those who are sanctified in Jesus Christ—who are the saints. That such is his view is proved by his statement that Che Guevara was an authentic martyr. As to love, his conception of it is very far from the love Paul speaks of in the thirteenth chapter of Corinthians. Writes Father Maillard: "We might be shocked at some of the methods of constraint [violent constraint!] applied to those who oppose the policy of the nation.* But we must not incontinently condemn the constrainers. They are wise. We must not impede the global revolution of our brothers by our scruples. We face a real choice. Love in the form of generosity must be rejected as too idyllic; authentic love comes through political, economic, sociological studies.† We must love man on the level of his social betterment." I agree that Father Maillard rightly objects to certain elements in what Christians have called love—affectation, niggardliness, mediocrity. Unhappily, fighting error with error and lies with lies is not a sound procedure. Moreover, unlike some of the other theologians who hold that violence is necessary, Father Maillard is not concerned to show either that violence is consonant with Christian love or that there is a relation between Christianity and revolution.

Here we come to the most interesting part of his thought. He considers it false to pretend that Christian premisses lead to the conclusion that there is a revolutionary tendency or force in the Christian message; he considers it equally false

---

* Once more we find here a justification of dictatorship (but which?) and identification of the revolutionary party with the "nation."

† Unfortunately, I must say that the studies in various issues of *Frères du Monde* (from which these quotations are taken) seem to me very weak from a political and sociological point of view.

to say that obedience requires participation in revolution. What is required is simply that we support revolution, for revolution is a value in itself. Why does Father Maillard draw a line between Christianity and revolution when, as we have seen, all the other theologians of revolution try to show that the two are connected and that Christianity motivates revolution? Father Maillard says he thinks this attitude is in fact an expression of the wish on the part of Christians to "recapture" the revolution. Others started it and carried it on; then Christians try to appropriate it into their system, in order to give it value; and this is dishonest. Revolution is the act of men, and men must be granted the credit for their acts. Christians have nothing to contribute to revolution. What they are after—whether by deducing a revolutionary idea from the gospel or by creating a theology of revolution—is to capture the revolution for their own benefit, to adorn themselves with the name and acts of others. And so, Father Maillard continues, they put revolution on the wrong track and change its meaning. Indeed some elements of the gospel—e.g., love—will necessarily weaken, devitalize revolution. Therefore, as he sees it, all the Christian need do is just keep quiet about his Christianity and join in revolution simply as a man, on the human level, without dragging in Christian motivations. This extreme position has at least the merit of honesty; and Father Maillard does not share the mania of many Christians to "justify" what happens in the world (a matter we shall take up farther on).

But why, then, participate in revolution? Father Maillard answers—not in so many words but *implicitly*—that after all, revolution is a value in itself. True men participate in revolution, and revolution begets the hope of a liberated humanity. So revolution is the only way a man, as a man, can take. Revolution has all the marks of an absolute value, it needs no motivations.

Moreover, if the Christian aligns himself with revolution, he will always find a basic response. Let me underline the reversal that occurs here: it is not because he is a Christian that a man must participate in revolution, *but* if he aligns himself with it, he will, as a Christian, find a great reward; namely, authentic encounter with the other. For there is no true encounter except through total involvement, without reservation. Thus it is only if, disregarding the reservations his faith might dictate, a Christian surrenders himself to revolution—an absolute that makes total demands on all who work in it and therefore involves total encounter among them—it is only then that the Christian encounters the other, and also encounters God. For Father Maillard's position (like Father Cardonnel's) is necessarily close to that of the death-of-God theologians. God cannot be perceived except in the encounter with the neighbor. I shall deal with this matter later, along with other theological consequences of this revolutionary doctrine. Here I merely indicate that a theory of revolution necessarily comes out of the death-of-God theology.

THE CHARACTER OF CHRISTIAN
PARTICIPATION IN VIOLENCE

Christians who participate in violence are generally of a distressingly simplistic cast of mind. Invariably, they judge socio-political problems on the basis of stereotyped formulas which take no account of reality. Indeed, the appeal to violence indicates incapacity to grasp the actual problems and incapacity to act. This is a far cry from the thought of Georges Sorel, who, in his *Reflections on Violence*, made a genuine analysis of the world of 1910 and examined in depth the meaning of violence. Instead, today's Christian theologians and intellectuals are sadly "primarist." Suddenly, they see participation in violence as the universal solution. They do not even stop to consider that when the violence is over, few if any problems will have been resolved and the real problems will arise. (Remember what happened to Pancho Villa after he attained power.) The simplicism of these people reminds me of a Nazi's statement: "When I come up against intellectuals who pose a problem, I kill the intellectuals; then there is no more problem." It is quite understandable that a man in the throes of anger or discouragement should think there is nothing left except a violent explosion. Thus a nervous father gives his son a box on the ear and, having released his nervous tension, imagines he has settled the question the boy asked. Examples of this simplicism abound—for instance, the views of Canon Gonzalez Ruiz.* He thinks not only that the Christian faith stimulates the development of socialism (an arguable idea), but also that revolution, which is to say violence, can solve all of society's problems. But he does not analyze those problems with any thoroughness.

Simplicism is also well represented in the United States. I cite a few examples at random. "Sense and Psychedelics," an editorial report appearing in the November 15, 1967, issue of *The Christian Century*, shows how widespread the temptation to violence is in Christian circles. Kyle Haselden, the late editor of the journal, explains that at a conference on Church and Society, convened by the National Council of Churches, one of the so-called "work groups" declared that American society is guilty of overt violence against the poor and maintains an unacceptable order of injustice, and that

---

* Gonzalez Ruiz: "Les chrétiens et la révolution" (in Spanish), *Boletín de la H.O.A.C.*, February, 1967 (Fraternité ouvrière de l'action catholique).

the church supports this exploitation by its own "systemic" violence. This is partially true, but simplistic. But the group drew remarkable conclusions from it. Haselden quotes from the group's statement:

When violence aimed at systemic violence occurs it ought to be defended, supported and interpreted in such a manner as will aid, hasten its end, and serve to establish a greater measure of justice. . . . In any conflict between the government and the oppressed or between the privileged classes and the oppressed, the church, for good or ill, must stand with the oppressed. . . . Systemic violence [that of the church and other organizations] may be violently confronted by its main victims as well as by others on their behalf. Those who adopt such tactics should seek a clear understanding of the requirements for making it effective. . . . Detailed mobilization of church resources must be developed to respond to confrontation between the police-military arm of the state and subjugated, robbed and excluded populations.

Haselden comments on this statement as follows:

The members of the group that issued these statements are neither as harmless as doves nor as wise as serpents. To suggest to the churches, which, Negro as well as white, are already deeply involved in covert violence in this country and overt violence abroad, that they should violently take up arms against violence —that is, against themselves—is the height of political naïveté. And to say as these doubleminded absolutists did that as Christians we must oppose violence in Vietnam but use violence in the United States, that Christians must support the oppressed in *any* conflict with the government, that violence can be baptized in the name of Jesus Christ, that nothing will save our society short of total revolution, is to indulge in loose and irresponsible talk that is not only unchristian but politically stupid. More violence is undoubtedly on the way in this country. The church and the state are by default of duty guaranteeing that calamity. But when

Christians preach the saving power of violence they, too, contribute to the terror and the evil of our time.*

This seems a very balanced judgment. I want to emphasize, however, that in another issue (January 17, 1968) *The Christian Century* published a very favorable review of two books that exalt violence—the one by Regis Debray, the other by Frantz Fanon. (Both books were originally published in France.) The reviewer not only demands that his readers think seriously about violence; he clearly approves of Fanon's proclamations, not realizing how terribly superficial and incantatory they are.

However, few in the United States go as far as Thomas Q. Melville, the Roman Catholic priest who, it seems, wants to assume the mantle of Camilo Torres. I think it important to quote from a report on Father Melville that appeared in *Le Monde* (February 21, 1968):

> In a letter he sent to the Mexican daily *La Prensa*, the American Catholic priest Thomas Q. Melville, a member of the Maryknoll Society who had been expelled from Guatemala the preceding December because, it was charged, he had aided the guerrillas, bases his approval of the guerrillas' action on the encyclical *Populorum progressio* and on a pastoral letter issued the previous year by the conference of Guatemala's bishops.
>
> The situation existing in Guatemala, Father Melville writes, is exactly the kind of situation which, the encyclical admits, is the exception that justifies recourse to violence: a situation "of obvious and prolonged tyranny which gravely violates the basic human rights of the human person."
>
> The American priest also bases his defense of the guerrillas' right to revolt on the episcopal letter which analyzes the situation obtaining in Guatemala. He cites passages from this letter:

* Kyle Haselden, in *The Christian Century*, November 15, 1967. Copyright © 1967 by The Christian Century Foundation. Used with permission.

"No one can deny that our social and economic reality is terribly unjust and unbalanced, that change in our vitiated structures is mandatory, and that it is necessary first of all to change the mentality of our fellow citizens.

"The inequitable distribution of the national revenue; the disparity in the scale of salaries (some dispose of emoluments which are an insult to the poverty of the country, while the immense majority receives a miserable pittance); the fact that a bare two per cent of the active population owns seventy per cent of the arable land; the system of recruiting our agricultural laborers, who do not even enjoy legal status; the fact that hundreds of thousands of school-age children lack basic education; the disintegration of the family; the growing immorality everywhere—all this demands bold and definitive change."

"Is not this," asks Father Melville, "a case of obvious and prolonged tyranny? If the situation described by the Guatemalan bishops (who indeed are not fully aware of all the evils rife in the country) is not a tyranny, then I say that St. Peter has spoken in vain and that the situation he describes does not exist anywhere."

Finally, the Maryknoll religious says, while the church perhaps did not approve the Crusades, the two world wars, the Korean war, or today's Vietnam war, the fact that it did not condemn them "shows that it accepts the idea that there can be a just war, and that men might sometimes be right in taking up arms to defend themselves." "The United States," Father Melville continues, "supports the Guatemalan army in order to maintain the status quo. If that support ceased, perhaps armed conflict would not even be needed to end the present state of affairs. . . . The present situation is in no sense an accident of history; it is a deliberate perversion of the natural order by a minority, supported, with the blessing of the Catholic hierarchy, by the national army which in turn is supported by the American government."

Father Melville then tells how he and two other members of his society, a nun and a priest, were accused of aiding Guatemala's guerrillas. "We never aided them," he writes; "we simply attended a meeting in the course of which they explained their point of view to us. . . . When we wanted to help the miserable masses we came up against indifference and even opposition on the part of the government." And he concludes: "When we were expelled we decided in favor of the guerrillas."

These examples suffice to show that we are dealing with the same simplification of the problem of the Christian's presence in the world and of the politico-social questions of our time—though the above descriptions of the situation obtaining in Guatemala seems indeed to be accurate.

Christians who favor revolution say that they must do so because a new situation has arisen, owing to the existence of capitalism and imperialism. As they see it, their attitude represents an innovation in Christianity, an acknowledgment of the duty, imposed by faith, to be in the midst of men, and a response to the opening given Christianity for witness in the modern world. The first part of their analysis is radically inaccurate. I am now referring to the doctrinaires and the theologians. I wrote about them above and showed that the tendency toward violence has always existed in Christianity. Here I am speaking of Christians who actually participate in violence. Well, this, too, has always existed. I shall not mention Münzer again. But, for example, in Spain, in the time of Napoleon I, the popular war against the imperial armies was led largely by village pastors, who headed the partisans and the guerrillas.

Again, Fouché, in his *Mémoires*, reports that the clergy led the resistance to Napoleon in Italy (1811). Priests sounded the call to violence. And in the Viterbo campaigns, Pastor Battaglia, putting himself at the head of a rebel band, fought the "imperialists" and spread terror among those who collaborated with the French. In other words, in the course of history priests have often adopted an attitude that many nowadays think is new and quite naturally stood with their flock. Thus recourse to violence is no invention of present-day Christians, no innovation. Nor is it a phenomenon linked with the development of capitalism and imperialism. In fact, in every epoch the Christians who went along with violent movements did it (certainly not because they were Christians) because they shared the dominant ideology of their society. Fifty years ago, it would never have occurred to Christians to favor such movements. But today, it is fair to say, the dominating ideology everywhere is a socializing, anti-colonialist ideology, and "advanced" Christians fall in line and march along on the road of violence. They adopt the nationalist ideology—exactly as in 1810-1815.

This bit of history prompts both a question and the answer to it. The Christians who supported those guerrilla movements back in 1810-1815—were they giving a Christian witness, were they serving either Christianity or man? And those pastors in Spain and Italy—did they bring their people closer to Christianity, did they witness to Jesus Christ, did they serve man? Alas, considering what were the ultimate consequences of their nationalist ideology, it cannot be said that it benefited man. This is a point that is extremely important. It shows how vain are enterprises like that of Camilo Torres and indeed of all who are tempted by violence. They pay a very high price—their life—for nothing; and they carry others along on the road of bitterness and hatred—passions that certainly do not exemplify Christian truth. I must say once more that these Christians shared the dominant ideology of their time.

Today, Christians justify their involvement in violence by declaring that they are motivated by love of the poor. Now love of the poor undoubtedly represents a truly Christian attitude and is indeed an important element in the orientation analyzed above. Unfortunately, the writings of these Christian proponents of violence raise suspicion as to their professions about the poor. The fact is that they are not con-

cerned for the poor—not for all the poor! Theirs is a selective
attitude: there are the poor who are worthy of being loved—
and then there are the others. Of course, these Christians do
not say anything that cynical. They declare their love of the
poor, explain the necessity of using violence in behalf of the
poor, and then cite only *one* category of the poor. There are
the "interesting" poor: the Negroes in the United States and
in South Africa, the North Vietnamese, the Vietcong, the
Palestinian Arabs, the poor of Latin America. And then there
are the "uninteresting" poor, people who obviously are not
worth troubling about: the Biafrans, massacred by the federal troops of Nigeria; the monarchist Yemenites, burned by
napalm and bombed into obliteration by the Egyptian air
force from 1964 to 1967; the South Sudanese, destroyed en
masse by the North Sudanese; the Tibetans, oppressed and
deported by China; the Khurds, perhaps 500,000 of whom
were massacred in Irak and Iran between 1955 and today.
These and many more in similar case do not attract the interest of our violent Christians.* Are they less poor than the
others? They are much poorer, because no one is concerned
for them. Why then are they ignored? Alas, the reason is
very simple. The interesting poor are those whose defense is
in reality an attack against Europe, against capitalism, against
the U.S.A. The uninteresting poor represent forces that are
considered passé. Their struggle concerns themselves only.
They are fighting not to destroy a capitalist or colonialist
regime, but simply to survive as individuals, as a culture, a
people. And that, of course, is not at all interesting, is it?
But the choice violent Christians make has nothing to do
with love of the poor. They choose to support this or that
group or movement because it is socialist, anti-colonialist,
anti-imperialist, etc.

---

* The frightful news of the genocide of the Patochos Indians in Brazil by
that country's Bureau of Indian Affairs scarcely roused interest among our
revolutionary Christians.

Now I have no objection whatever to socialism and so on, and I certainly grant that every person—and that means every Christian, too—has a right to support these causes. What I do object to is the hypocrisy of those who profess that their support is based on Christian principles. For a Christian to say that it is love of justice or love of the poor that prompts him to participate in such movements, is hypocrisy. The first rule for a Christian is truthfulness. If he freely admits that his participation is based not on Christian but on purely humane considerations, then I am content and have no more to say. He has accepted a secular ideology and, like Father Maillard, honestly admits as much. However, if he still holds to his faith in Jesus Christ, he will, sooner or later, necessarily encounter contradictions between that faith and that ideology.

But mind, I am not saying that the Christian should not feel concern for the poor man who is his neighbor and whose neighbor he is. On the contrary. It is obvious that for the Christian American the black American is "the poor"; and it is equally obvious that the Christian American must struggle with and for his black brothers. My criticism is directed at the universalizing and overly theoretical position of the intellectuals, theologians and politicians who proclaim that they are responsible for all the world's poor but in fact—perhaps without knowing it—are partisans and politicians.

Let me emphasize that recourse to violence is a sign of incapacity: incapacity to solve the fundamental questions of our time (perhaps even just to *see* them) and incapacity to discern the specific form Christian action ought to take. I repeat once more that I fully understand the insurrection of the oppressed who see no way out, who fight desperately against the violence done them and will break loose from their chains the moment they can. I fully understand the revolts of slaves, the violent workers' strikes of the nineteenth century, the rebellion of colonized peoples who want to avenge a century of humiliation, privation and injustice at one blow. I understand these explosions and, what is more, I *approve* of them. The oppressed have no other way of protesting their human right to live; and they think, too, that by rebelling they can change their situation for the better, if only to some small degree. But what cannot be condoned is that Christians associate themselves with this avengement, and, worse, that Christians affirm that violence will secure fundamental change. Christians do not have the reasons for believing this that the oppressed have. Christians ought above all to play the role of society's sentinel (Ezekiel), to interpret for society the meaning of acts and events. But, of course, that is much more difficult and much less exciting than to plunge thoughtlessly into revolutionary action.[*] To be on the side of the oppressed and at the same time have to tell them that their explosions of violence are futile and will bring no real change—this is the most thankless position anyone can take. It was the position of Martin Luther King, and we know how vulnerable it is. It was also the position of Jesus in relation to the Pharisees (who wanted to organize resistance to the Romans) and the Zealots.

Our prophets of violence indulge in revolutionary verbalism instead of trying seriously to determine what specifically Christian action is required. That indeed is very difficult to determine in a society as complex as ours. How express on the level of collective life the specific nature of the Christian life? What form must obedience take in our day

---

[*] M. G. MacGrath, Bishop of Panama, put it precisely (April, 1968): "The idealism and impatience of some of our best Christian leaders lay them open to the emotional appeal of the guerrilla heroes. But few are equipped with the tools for analyzing the ethical or even the tactical problems that violence involves."

and age? How show our contemporaries that the action of
Christ makes us new men, that is, different men? So far, all
attempts to answer these questions have been a total loss.
Social Christianity (which on the whole is simple socialism), the Bekenntnis Kirche (which, once Hitlerism was
defeated, merely aligned itself with anti-Hitlerism, thus with
what might be called socio-communism), the ideas of Rein-
hold Niebuhr (which, while solidly thought out, affected
neither church nor society)—all have failed. And the worst
failure is that of the World Council of Churches, which
regularly bypasses the *fundamental* problems of our time
and devotes its energies to the most superficial ones. The
ethical consequences of the faith have not been examined
with any theological depth, and the stupendous newness of
our society—a newness that renders all older conceptions
antiquated—has not been adequately analyzed. Christians
reject all such analysis as useless. Burning to do something,
to make themselves felt, to bear witness in the midst of men,
they rush headlong into action. No matter what action, provided only it be action, thus visible. That, they think, is
where men are, and that is enough. And then—since they
will not stop to consider how they might make a specifically
Christian contribution—they align themselves with the political, economic and social positions of these other movements. They forget that what men really need is not a few
more adherents for their movements, but something that
Christ alone offers: the specificity of the Christian message.
The Christian who accepts violence, like the Christian who
thinks he can ignore violence, has abdicated from Christianity as a way of life. He has given up the attempt to express
his faith in the difficult situation of today. Impatient with
theologians and ratiocinating intellectuals, he will give his
heart's allegiance to no matter what, and abandon himself
to the currents of the world.

THE THEOLOGICAL CONSEQUENCES

This attitude undoubtedly has a bearing on theology. I shall risk stating a hypothesis. Normally, it seems, knowledge and understanding of the Bible provide the basis for a theological view, which then provides the basis for right solution of all human problems and becomes an effective expression of the faith. Now, as we have seen, Christians who favor the use of violence do so "as a last resort"; that is, without thinking through the matter in theological terms, for they are convinced beforehand that there is no specifically Christian response to the world's problems. However, Christians cannot support violence if they feel that such support renders them liable to theological censure, if they feel that they are not doing the right thing. Thus acceptance of violence necessarily involves theological views; but these are formulated "after the fact," after the decision for violence has been taken. Then, however, the formulations themselves become justifications of the stance for violence. In the end, we fashion the theology we must have if we are to live with ourselves when we act as we do. We have rushed into violence because the current of society runs that way, because, good-hearted people that we are, we side with the oppressed. Now we must explain our stance in theological terms.

It seems to me that two aspects of the new theology bear out that statement. First, the tendency to reject reconciliation. I say this on the basis of close observation, for the partisans of violence insist that they are sincerely devoted to reconciliation. Many of them say that the world is reconciled to God right now. They ignore the negative judgments on the world to be found abundantly in the Gospels and

Epistles and take their stand on the text "God so loved the world. . . ." They go so far as to suggest that the church is not really important. It is the world that is important, the world that is saved; and it is in the world that God's love is disclosed. The church is only an accident, and it ought not to absorb Christians' strength and money. If the church exists, it exists only for the world or for others (the church's functions of praise and worship are forgotten). The church is meant for the world, because the world is the place where God acts. If pressed, these partisans will admit that the church is God's instrument in the world; but that is as far as they will go.

So reconciliation seems to occupy a prominent place in this line of thought. In fact, however, reconciliation is stressed only in order to justify the Christian's intervention in politics: since the world is reconciled (and under the Lordship of Jesus Christ), all its undertakings—political, technological, scientific, economic—are legitimate and claim everyone's participation. So runs the apologia of the proponants of violence. And up to this point they all agree. But when concrete action must be decided on, they disagree. For at this point—tacitly and perhaps unconsciously—the question of reconciliation comes up again. On the one hand, the world is reconciled to God; but on the other hand, not everything and everyone in the world shares in that reconciliation: there are still the wicked. And the wicked are identified: they are the capitalists, the racists, the colonialists, the fascists, the anti-communists; or else they are the Communists, Negroes, workers, liberals, anti-racists (for it must not be forgotten that if the socialist mood is dominant among Christian intellectuals in Europe, the opposite is the case in the United States; and both sides have been infected by violence). There can be no reconciliation with the wicked of either group. The Bible speaks of the reconciliation of the wicked to God, and of loving your enemies (that is, people you consider wicked); but precisely that aspect of God's work is excluded here. So "reconciliation of the world" is interpreted: "The world" means "the things I like in the world —science, technology, etc.," and that "world" is reconciled. And "reconciliation of men" means "of the men whose political opinions I agree with." Thus Christian support of violence implies the monstrous theological sequel that revolution is *prerequisite* to reconciliation. Revolution will be the prelude to reconciliation, to the development of a new humanity. To preach reconciliation in the context of the old economic and political structures is hypocrisy. What is needed is new structures, and these cannot be created save by revolutionary means.

This view is just as emphatically advanced by right-wingers as by left-wingers. The Ku Klux Klan and the South African racialists cite the Bible in defense of their attitude. But in fact their attitude is the same as their opponents'. They deny that all men are reconciled in Jesus Christ; they deny that reconciliation, if it means anything, means reconciliation with the enemy and with everyone else.

Christian proponents of violence go so far as to say that the theology of reconciliation is a vestige of the past, an effort to perpetuate things as they are and to forestall change. In the Bible, they insist, reconciliation does not obtain universally. Yahweh and the Baalim are totally opposed to each other; the prophets shouted out condemnations; the disciples did not preach reconciliation until after Jesus' death and resurrection. Strangely, the authors of these arguments apparently do not notice that the Bible says the opposite of what they say it does. According to the Bible, there is no reconciliation with false gods, with idols, with the powers that rule the world, with "the world" as it is; but there *is* reconciliation with all men. The crucifixion and the resurrection signalize the defeat of the powers (which nowadays wear the form of money, the state, productivity, science, technology, etc.), but not of men. But alas, the violence espoused by so many modern Christians is always directed against men. Negroes must be punished, capitalists must be expropriated, etc. How is it that they cannot see that to reject the theology of reconciliation in favor of the theology of revolution is in fact to reject the Incarnation?

In this connection let me repeat once again that it does not matter so much that "Christians" participate in violence, that they massacre blacks or whites. But it matters greatly that they profess to do it for "Christian" reasons and insist that they are only trying to clear the way for a new Christian social order. "To reconciliation through violent revolution" is the most hypocritical of slogans, and those who mouth it reveal their ignorance of the most elementary Christian truths.

The second theological consequence of the violent stance is even more radical—nothing less than the theology of the death of God. I shall not here analyze the various branches of this theology, its points of view and its results. In these pages I limit myself to presenting a kind of sociology of theology. But it is perhaps useful to say at once that very often the theology of revolution and the death-of-God theology are generated in the same circles, among the same groups of Christians. Sometimes indeed the theologians of one or other of them declare that these two theologies go hand in hand. They are right. As we have seen, Father Maillard is of the opinion that there can be no encounter with God except through the person of the other; and he adds that the idea of a personal, transcendent God is untenable. The idea of transcendence, he says, belongs to the infancy of the human race and is on the same level with the bourgeois idea of a hierarchical society. On his part, Father Cardonnel is the great theorist of "horizontal relations." Any idea of "verticality"—that is, relation with a God existing on a higher level than man—must be rejected. "From now on," he says, "God exists only in downtrodden people; that is what God's transcendence amounts to."*

Let me point out also that there is a connection between the death-of-God theology and rejection of the theology of reconciliation; and this rejection, as we have said, is in fact denial of the Incarnation. The same problem is raised by the death-of-God theology. If there is no such God as the Old Testament reveals, then there is no incarnation; for if there is no God, then who or what could be incarnate in the person of Jesus? All that remains is the person of Jesus, in whom we see the only possible God (obviously, there is no reference here to that old theological formula of the "two natures," which is dismissed as a medieval relic). But this Jesus is only a human being, and (as Pastor Ennio Flores has well put it) if he is God it is only because he is the poorest of men. Thus every encounter with a poor person is also an encounter with Jesus Christ and God. But "God" is a meaningless term. However, it is clear that the revolutionary stance and its various theological consequences are of a piece.

Now let me go further and show that the theology of violence both implies and derives from the theology of the death of God. A theology of violence calls for discrimination for or against certain men or groups of men; therefore it *must* deny the Father who loves all men equally. The ar-

* It is true that, commenting on his own famous formula, "God is dead in Jesus Christ," Father Cardonnel explains that the God who is dead is the autocratic, arbitrary, despotic God, the ruler of a world that automatically produces rich and poor people. "The Lord who took the character of a slave could not have had a despotic father." All of which seems to me to indicate a curious misunderstanding of the whole Bible.

gument—a fallacious one, to be sure—is that man "come of age" has no need of God, or that psychoanalytic doctrines have rendered God obsolete. But the real motivation for getting rid of God is to be found deep in the unconscious. The Christian, eager to participate in public life, chooses to side for or against some group, his choice depending on his own class feelings and political and racial passions; and having taken sides he accepts the propaganda that stigmatizes every opponent as subhuman and an embodiment of evil. But this is an intolerable idea—*unless* we are no longer the children of one Father, unless the creation story is a mere myth, unless the "vertical relationship" (at once unique, personal and universal) no longer exists. When we all thought of each other as children of the same Father, we knew that war is a terrible evil. Now that God is dead, we can exploit creation to the utmost and defend mankind by killing all the people whose views of what man ought to be differ from ours. Of course, the death-of-God theologians contend with all their strength for an end of the Algerian war or the Vietnam war, but the only atrocities they can see are those committed by the party they condemn, the French or the Americans. Thus suppression of God permits love to be selective, partisan, capricious; for the only kind of relation left is the horizontal one.

Let us consider another aspect of this theology. The Bible tells us that it is God alone who establishes justice and God alone who will institute the kingdom at the end of time. It is true that some Christians have made this teaching an excuse for doing nothing; for since God is the guarantor and the founder of justice, the establishment of social justice can be left to him. But they *knew* that this was a wretched excuse, a shabby evasion. With the death of God, however, we can expect nothing from any source but ourselves. We ourselves must undertake to establish social justice. A position that is certainly courageous and, humanly speaking, valid. But who is to decide what justice is? How are we to discern justice? Many Christians refused to imitate the generations of theologians who have agonized over these questions. On the basis of the one biblical text they clung to (Matthew 25), they concluded that justice obviously consisted in feeding the poor, etc. Now this, too, is good theoretically. But we have seen that different groups of the poor are dealt with differently. Moreover, this conception of justice leads to assimilating the cause of the poor with socialism. So European Christians rush into the socialist camp in the belief that socialism assures justice. And then they accept the means socialism uses to establish justice— namely, the violent tactics described above. The theology of the death of God is meaningless save as it throws open the door for man to act without restraint and at the same time assures him that he is right in acting so; for it declares that the sole duty of human beings is to act—obviously, in human fashion—among their fellows on earth.

That is why I think it is no accident that this death-of-God theology grew out of two anterior developments: the discovery that Christians must participate in politics and in public affairs, and the justification of violence. But (and I choose my words carefully) if that is so, then this theology is not really a theology but an ideology. In spite of the impression some death-of-God writers may give, this line of thought is based not on the Revelation but altogether on philosophical considerations.

Here I shall merely enumerate the three characteristics that, in my opinion, mark an ideology as such. First, its premisses concerning society and modern man are pseudo-scientific: for example, the affirmation that man has become adult, that he no longer needs a Father, that the Father-God was invented when the human race was in its infancy, etc.;

the affirmation that man has become rational and thinks scientifically, and that therefore he must get rid of the religious and mythological notions that were appropriate when his thought processes were primitive; the affirmation that the modern world has been secularized, laicized, and can no longer countenance religious people, but if they still want to preach the kerygma they must do it in laicized terms; the affirmation that the Bible is of value only as a cultural document, not as the channel of Revelation, etc. (I say "affirmation" because these are indeed simply affirmations, unrelated either to fact or to any scientific knowledge about modern man or present-day society.) These various affirmations are matters of belief, based on misinterpretation of facts, misunderstanding of psychological and sociological discoveries, and, finally, on popular, commonly held notions. Now it is certainly one of the characteristics of an ideology that it presents as scientific truth what in reality is simply irrational belief.

The second characteristic of an ideology is that its real aims are quite different from those it announces. Some subject, a theological idea, is elucidated in the most serious way, not by any means in order to start a theological debate, but in order to confirm the feeling that a Christian must be active in the world. So this is no attempt to interpret the revealed truth more clearly (anyway, if God does not exist, whose would the revelation be?), but an ideological construct intended to promote an action that people feel the need of performing. This perversion of truly intellectual procedures is also an earmark of ideologies.

The third characteristic of an ideology is its justificatory purpose. The ultimate purpose of the whole death-of-God system is to justify a certain kind of behavior on the part of Christians in relation to society—a kind of behavior that is dictated by conformism to the modern world. So a justificatory formula is manufactured; and alas, it often turns out that theology merely amounts to a justification of the behavior of pretend-Christians. The theology of the death of God reinforces this evil tendency. It justifies a sociological impulsion. That is the kind of theology it really is, unconsciously. Nor do the marvelous intellectual operations its proponents perform with every appearance of seriousness make it less profoundly false.

Such are the theological consequences of Christians' defense of violence. They are grave consequences.

3

Christian Realism
in the Face of Violence

IF WE want to find out what the Christian attitude toward violence should be, we cannot proceed by deducing the consequences of Christian principles or by enumerating biblical texts. The Bible does frequently condemn violence, but it defends violence just as frequently—even in the New Testament. So this is not a good method of seeking an answer to our question. I believe that the first thing the Christian must do in relation to problems of social ethics is to be completely realistic, to get as clear and exact an understanding of the facts as possible. Realism is the necessary basis for Christian thinking on society. (Of course, I am not now referring to philosophical or metaphysical realism.) By realism I mean two things: first, seeing the facts as they are and grasping them thoroughly, without evasion or illusion, without recoiling in fear or horror as it becomes evident what the result of some trend is likely to be. Surely the Christian—and only the Christian—should be able to exercise this clarity of vision and thought because the Revelation has to some degree given him an understanding of the world, and also because, terrible as the reality may be, he can accept it without despairing, for he has hope in Jesus Christ. In his examination of the facts the Christian must not yield to emotional urges, however justified they may seem (the urge to help the poor, for instance). "You shall not change your judgment according to whether your brother is rich or poor" (Leviticus 19:15), and expressly, "You shall not be partial to a poor man in his suit" (Exodus 23:3). But also: "You shall not attack the rights of the poor" (Exodus 23:6). To say, however, that reality must not be approached with a bias toward the poor is certainly not to say that the rich should be favored. On the contrary!

Second, Christian realism means knowing clearly what one is doing. Naturally I do not deny that the Holy Spirit may intervene and give direction to our action; but the possibility of the Spirit's intervention is no justification for rushing pell-mell into action, just for the sake of action; for yielding to some emotion, sentiment, visceral reaction, on the plea that "God will turn it to account" or, worse, in the conviction that this visceral reaction is tantamount to a divine commandment or a prophetic insight. Christian realism demands that a man understand exactly what he is doing, why he is doing it, and what the results of his doing will be. The Christian can never act spontaneously, as though he were an Illuminist. He must be harmless as the dove (the sacrificial victim, ready to sacrifice himself in his action—for the dove is the sacrificial victim) and wise as the serpent (that is, fully aware of just what he thinks and does). He must use the light of reason, of science and technology, to get his bearings, for the "children of this world are wiser than we." He must be the careful architect who, in accordance with Jesus' advice, sits down to work out plans and calculate the cost before starting to build. All of which is to say that, contrary to widely held opinion, faith in the Holy Spirit does not mean that we may act imprudently, close our eyes and refuse to think; rather, it means that we must use our heads and try

to see with clarity. True, the Holy Spirit—who is clarity itself—may propel us into the greatest imprudence; but then
we shall know it.

So the Christian who wants to find out what he ought to
do must be realistic; this is the first step. It goes without saying, however, that he must reject a great deal of what the
world calls "realism." He may study and analyze the facts,
but he will not make them the basis of his action, he will not
be ruled by reality. Realism, as generally understood, leads
to the conclusion that "things being as they are, this is the
realistic line to take." The Christian must indeed see things
as they are, but he will not derive his principles of action
from them. This realism gives him a clear idea of what the
choices are in the given situation, but he will not take the
action that is automatically indicated—though he will be
tempted to do so; for reality, once seen, is hard to escape from.

Moreover, Christian realism will prevent self-approbation
for what we do; when we calculate the probable results of
our actions in a rational manner, we are not at all likely to
be proud of ourselves or to praise our works; rather, Christian realism leads to humility. But anyone who is not realistic in this sense is like the blind leading the blind in the
parable.

Now, I have been studying the problem of violence (especially violence as practiced today) for a long time, and on
several occasions have played some role in violent actions.
So I can state that what is most lacking in this regard among
my brother Christians is neither good will nor charity, neither
concern for justice nor dedication, neither enthusiasm nor
willingness to make sacrifices—none of these; what is lacking
is realism. Where violence is concerned, Christians generally
behave like imbecile children. And I do not believe that stupidity is a Christian virtue. On the other hand, intelligence

is obviously not an absolute requirement, but realism as I have tried to define it *is*. I shall cite only one text: "But Jesus did not trust himself to them, . . . for he knew what was in man" (John 2:24-25)—though this certainly did not keep him from giving his life for these same men!

VIOLENCE AS NECESSITY

Consequently, the first thing the Christian must do regarding violence is to perceive exactly what violence is. And rigorous realism requires going far beyond the usual generalities; for the natural man fools himself about fact, cannot bear to look at a situation as it is, invents stories to cover up reality. Yet it must be recognized that violence is to be found everywhere and at all times, even where people pretend that it does not exist. Elsewhere I have shown in detail that every state is founded on violence and cannot maintain itself save by and through violence.* I refuse to make the classic distinction between violence and force. The lawyers have invented the idea that when the state applies constraint, even brutal constraint, it is exercising "force"; that only individuals or nongovernmental groups (syndicates, parties) use violence. This is a totally unjustified distinction. The state is established by violence—the French, American, Communist, Francoist revolutions. Invariably there is violence at the start. And the state is legitimized when the other states recognize it (I know that this is not the usual criterion of legitimacy, but it is the only real one!). Well then, when is a state recognized? When it has lasted for a tolerable length of time. During the state's early years the world

* See my *L'illusion politique*. Space will not permit me to repeat this long argument here. English edition, *Political Illusion* (New York: Knopf, 1967).

is scandalized that it was established by violence, but presently the fact is accepted, and after a few years it is recognized as legitimate (cf. the Communist, Hitler, Franco states). What puzzles everyone today is that Mao's China has not been accorded such formal recognition.

Now how does a government stay in power? By violence, simply by violence. It has to eliminate its enemies, set up new structures; and that, of course, can be done only by violence. And even when the situation seems to be normalized, the government cannot endure except by repeated exercise of violence. Where is the line between police brutality and brutality exercised by others? Is the difference that the former is legal? But it is common knowledge that laws can be so drawn up as to justify violence. The Nuremberg judgments are obviously the best example in point. The Nazi chiefs had to be got rid of. Good enough. This was a violent reaction against violence. The perpetrators of violence were defeated and vengeance had to be visited upon them. But democratic scruples prompted the declaration that this was not a case of violence but of justice. However, there were no laws under which the Nazi chiefs could be condemned. So a special law was invented, a law condemning genocide, etc. And so those Nazis could be condemned by a formal court in good conscience, because this was a case of justice, not of violence. Of course, the world knew that Stalin had done the same things as Hitler—genocide, deportation camps, torture, summary executions. But Stalin was not defeated. So he could not be condemned. In his case it was simply a question of violence.

Domestically, too, the state uses violence. Before it does anything else it must establish order—such is the first great rule for states. But this—at least at the beginning—means order in the streets, not legal order. For there can be no lawful constraint, based on justice, save when the situation is relatively calm, when citizens obey the laws and order actually reigns. But so long as it faces crisis or encounters obstacles, the state does what it considers necessary, and following the Nuremberg procedure it enacts special laws to justify action which in itself is pure violence. These are the "emergency laws," applicable while the "emergency" lasts. Every one of the so-called civilized countries knows this game. In short, what we have here is ostensible legality as a cover for actual violence. And this masked violence is found at all levels of society. Economic relations, class relations, are relations of violence, nothing else. Truly, we must see things as they are and not as we imagine them to be or wish they were.

The competition that goes with the much-touted system of free enterprise is, in a word, an economic "war to the knife," an exercise of sheer violence that, so far, the law has not been able to regulate. In this competition "the best man wins"—and the weaker, more moral, more sensitive men necessarily lose. The system of free competition is a form of violence that must be absolutely condemned. But it would be foolish to suppose that planning will do away with violence; for then the state will implacably impose its rules on the enterprisers. We need only look about, even in France, to see to how great a degree planning involves calculations as to what must be sacrificed. This group of producers, that kind of exploitation are swept away, in accordance with economic estimates. And the Plan that requires these holocausts to the God of Economics is no less violent for being voted by a parliament and being made a law.

The same holds with respect to classes. I am well aware that one school of American sociologists says there is no such thing as social classes. I think their devotion to a pseudo-scientific method blinds them to the facts. However, their view is on the way out.* Certainly it is a fact that the relation between classes is one of violent competition for positions of power in the nation, for "a bigger slice of the cake"—that is, of the national revenue. How could it be otherwise? How could anyone suppose that the lower class—the workers, employees, peasants—will unprotestingly accept the dominance of the upper class—bourgeois, capitalist, bureaucratic, technocratic or whatever? And in any case the lower classes want to get control themselves. I do not want to revive the general "theory" of class war. I am not referring to that, but to the relations of violence that develop as soon as there is a hierarchy. The violence done by the superior may be physical (the most common kind, and it provokes hostile moral reaction), or it may be psychological or spiritual, as when the superior makes use of morality and even of Christianity to inculcate submission and a servile attitude; and this is the most heinous of all forms of violence. Communism's propaganda methods are psychological violence (or "psychological terrorism," as we call it in France). And indeed no hierarchy can maintain itself without using such violence. But, as Sorel's analysis so thoroughly demonstrates, once the lower class is no longer domesticated (in the sense that animals are domesticated), it nurses its resentment, envy and hatred—the leaven of violence.

Wherever we turn, we find society riddled with violence. Violence is its natural condition, as Thomas Hobbes saw clearly. The individual, he realized, had to be protected against violence. Starting out from this premiss, he came to the conclusion that only an absolute, all-powerful state, itself

* See, for example, Leonard Reissman, *Class in American Society* (New York: Macmillan, 1959).

using violence, could protect the individual against society's violence. In support of Hobbes's conclusion I could cite a vast company of modern sociologists and philosophers. I shall cite only two—men who are well known in France and represent quite different points of view. Ricoeur: "Nonviolence forgets that history is against it."* For history is made by violence. E. Weil: "War is the only force that can lift the individual above himself. . . . On the level of reality, the good is impotent; all power is on the side of evil."† I can attest that reality is indeed like that. But it is easier, more pleasant, more comforting, more moral and pious to believe that violence has been properly reprimanded and carefully hidden in a corner—to believe that kindness and virtue will always triumph. Unfortunately, that is an illusion.

After two centuries of optimistic idealism, violence arose in the U.S.A. That is to say, during those two centuries the nation refused to face reality and piously threw a veil over the facts. I shall not point to Negro slavery, as most critics of America do. I refer rather to the slow, sanctimonious extermination of the Indians, the system of occupying the land (*Faustrecht*), the competitive methods of the leading capitalist groups, the annexation of California along with the retrieval of Texas—all this and much besides show that the United States has always been ridden by violence, though the truth was covered over by a legalistic ideology and a moralistic Christianity. Americans have it that the Civil War was an accidental interruption of what was practically an idyllic state of affairs; actually, that war simply tore the veil

* *Revue esprit,* 1949.
† *L'état,* Paris, 1964.

off reality for a moment. Tocqueville saw the facts clearly.*
He indicated all the factors showing that the United States
was in a situation of violence which, he predicted, would
worsen. As a matter of fact, a tradition of violence is discern-
ible throughout United States history—perhaps because it
is a young nation, perhaps because it plunged into the industrial age without preparation. (This tradition, incidentally, explains the popularity of violence in the movies.)
And it seems that the harsher and more violent the reality
was, the more forcefully were moralism and idealism
affirmed.† Today, Americans are stunned when the world

---

* Let me quote Tocqueville directly. He describes the effects of the white
man's coming on nature, wildlife, etc., then explains the forms this legal
violence took: "In our time the Indians are being dispossessed step by step
and, one might say, altogether legally. . . . I believe that the Indian is condemned to perish, and I cannot but think that by the time the European
has settled the Pacific coast the Indians will no longer exist. . . . Isolated in
their own land, they have been a small colony of troublesome strangers in
the midst of a numerous and dominating people. . . . The states extended
what they called the 'benefit' of their laws to the Indians, calculating that
the Indians would go away rather than submit. And the central government
promised those unfortunates an asylum in the west, knowing that it could
not guarantee its promises. . . . The Spaniards, though (to their eternal
shame) they perpetrated unparalleled horrors on the Indians, could not ex-
terminate them, could not even deny them some rights. But the Americans
of the U.S. accomplished both these things, and in the cleverest way imaginable—calmly, legally, philanthropically, without bloodshed and, so far as the
world could see, without violating a single great moral principle. It would
be impossible to think of a better way of destroying people and at the same
time exhibiting higher respect for the laws of humanity." (*Democracy in
America*, Volume II, Chapter 10, paragraph 2.) All this is very far from the
right to the pursuit of happiness.

† In November, 1967, Father Arrupe, general of the Society of Jesus,
presented a remarkable analysis of the deep moral and religious roots of violence in the U.S.A. At the same time he outlined a reasonable program of
action against racial discrimination, basing his recommendations on the experience of the Jesuit order in the field.

rewards their good will and their sense of responsibility with revilement. But that is because they have never looked reality in the face and have based their international policies on a superficial idealism.* They are stunned at Negro violence, etc. The truth is that the United States is in an explosive situation—a complex situation whose elements are racialism, poverty (as the Americans understand it), and urban growth involving the disintegration of communities (the phenomenon of the metropolis). But for decades Americans have had the idea that every problem could be solved by law and good will. So in this case, too, idealism, refusing to recognize the latent violence, paved the way for the violence that has now broken out. I believe that Saul Bernstein, for instance, analyzes the situation altogether too simply when he ascribes the revolts of 1964-1966 to poverty, frustration, and bitterness.† On the basis of his analysis, he proposes solutions that are quite as inadequate as those that France proposed to the National Liberation Front in 1957. For Bernstein does not fully understand the significance, the universality, and the law of violence.

In writing this I certainly do not mean to indict the United States. I merely want to point out that even so moralized and Christianized a society, a society that holds to an admirable ideology of law and justice, and conducts psychological research on adaptation, etc.—even such a society is basically violent, like every other.

* A basic example: American pressure and American anticolonialist idealism forced the colonizing nations—first the Dutch, then the French in Vietnam—to make a "catastrophic" withdrawal. The result was that soon after, the Americans were obliged to intervene indirectly in Indonesia and directly in Vietnam. Thus their involvement in the Vietnam war is the direct consequence of their action in disarming France while she was fighting in Vietnam.

† Saul Bernstein: *Alternatives to Violence: Alienated Youth and Riots, Race and Poverty* (New York: Association Press, 1967).

Is this a "Christian" statement? It is indeed. For the courage to see this derives from the courage a man acquires through faith and hope in Jesus Christ. But something remains to be said. Granted, violence is universal. But also, violence is of the order of Necessity. I do not say violence is *a* necessity, but rather that a man (or a group) subject to the *order* of *Necessity** follows the given trends, be these emotional, structural, sociological, or economic. He ceases to be an independent, initiating agent; he is part of a system in which nothing has weight or meaning; and (this is important) so far as he obeys these inescapable compulsions he is no longer a moral being.

I must emphasize that, from two points of view, the order of violence cannot be brought under moral judgment. The man who practices violence cannot pretend to be acting as a moral being and in the name of some value; and the outsider cannot validly pass moral judgment on that violence— such a judgment would be meaningless. Sorel indeed attempts to work out an ethic based on violence, but obviously he fails. And our moralists who address the practitioner of violence in the name of virtue or religion or the good are indulging in meaningless behavior. The order of violence is like the order of digestion or falling bodies or gravitation. There is no sense in asking whether gravitation is a good thing or a bad one. If "nature" were not a much misunderstood term, and especially if there were not so many people (those, namely, who paved the way for the reign of violence) who actually believe that Nature is beneficent, I would say that what we have here is an expression of Nature. Gandhi said as much when he declared that violence is "the law of the brute."

---

* I use this term rather than "fatality," which has philosophical connotations. Besides, it might be objected that Jesus Christ overcame Fatality. But Necessity is always with us.

I am not saying that violence is an expression of *human* nature. I am saying, for one thing, that violence is the general rule for the existence of societies—including the societies that call themselves civilized but have only camouflaged violence by explaining and justifying it and putting a good face on it. I am saying also that when a man goes the way of violence he enters a system of necessities and subjects both himself and others to it. For such is the necessity in this world. Curiously enough, those who, nowadays, justify violence almost always argue that it is necessary. Many a time I have been told: "But after all, when a poor or unemployed man has nothing, nonviolence is useless, it cannot help him; only violence can. He *has* to use violence." It is certainly true that when a man suffers severe poverty or humiliation, rage is the only expression left him. But in giving way to his rage he should realize that he is acting on the animal level and is obeying a necessity; that he is not free. Again, the champions of the oppressed tell us: "Things being what they are, can anyone believe that true civic order can be established, that there can be genuine dialogue with the enemy? Dialogue demands that both parties be in a position to speak and reason with each other. But we who side with the poor—what resources do we command?" Violence! "Some people are incorrigible"—that is, the rich, the powerful, who "have fallen so low that love does not touch them. . . . In politics, it is difficult to make an alliance with the saint, the pure-hearted, and particularly difficult for the poor, whose rightful impatience urges them on." Thus Father Marcel Cornelis.* So, he adds, there is only one remedy for the ills of the poor: violence. Father Maillard agrees: "It is always the violence of the oppressor that unleashes the violence of the oppressed.

* "La non-violence et les pauvres," in *Cahiers de la réconciliation*, Paris, 1967.

The time comes when violence is the *only possible* way for the poor to state their case."

All this amounts to an acknowledgment of violence as necessity. And indeed violence is not only the means the poor use to claim their rights; it is also the sole means available to those in places of power. Jesus Christ told us what the order of this world is like: "You know that the rulers of the Gentiles lord it over them, and their great men exercise authority over them" (Matthew 20:25). And Jesus did not protest against this situation. Let us be clear about this: the text from Matthew refers not only to the chiefs of a legally established government (kings, etc.) or the controllers of wealth (bankers, etc.) but to all who come into positions of leadership. And there is no way for them to keep their power except by violence. All of them are *megaloi*, obsessed with grandiose ideas, whether they be leaders of the proletariat or revolutionary movements, or notables in the field of economics or science. All of them are subject to the same necessity: to tyrannize over and use others; that is, they are subject to the order of violence, which is a necessity. But "necessity" means "law." There is a law of violence.

THE LAW OF VIOLENCE

Realistic appraisal shows that violence is inevitable in all societies, whatever their form. This established, however, we must be equally realistic in examining the consequences. We grant that there is an inescapable law of violence, but we must be equally clear-sighted as to the results. It is disingenuous to say, "Violence is the only way open to us; but you'll see, the results will be excellent." Here the second aspect of Christian realism enters in: you must know what you are doing.

The first law of violence is continuity. Once you start using violence, you cannot get away from it. Violence expresses the habit of simplification of situations, political, social, or human. And a habit cannot quickly be broken. Once a man has begun to use violence he will never stop using it, for it is so much easier and more practical than any other method. It simplifies relations with the other completely by denying that the other exists. And once you have repudiated the other, you cannot adopt a new attitude—cannot, for example, start rational dialogue with him. Violence has brought so many clear and visible results; how then go back to a way of acting that certainly looks ineffectual and seems to promise only very doubtful results? So you go on using violence, even if at first you had thought that violence would be only a temporary expedient, even if you have achieved thorough change in your own or the general political situation. Mr. André Malraux, the government official, has a bodyguard of police armed with automatic pistols; the same Mr. Malraux, in the days when he was a revolutionary, carried an automatic himself. That, as we have seen, is the way with revolutions. They are born in violence and establish the reign of violence for a generation or two. Violence broke out in France in 1789, and continued, with a few interruptions, up to 1914, when it was mutated into world war. And the Marxist idealists are simply naïve when they believe that, once a reactionary government has been overthrown by violence, a just and peaceful regime will be established. Castro rules only by violence, Nasser and Boumedienne likewise; there is no difference at all between their regimes and the previous colonialist regimes that they ousted by violence. It is one of Mao's greatest merits that he has the courage frankly to repudiate socialist idealism and to see clearly that violence perpetuates itself. But he errs when he declares that a doctrine is involved here. The fact is that once violence is loosed, those who use it cannot get away from it.

The second law of violence is reciprocity. It is stated in Jesus' famous word, "*All* who take the sword will perish by the sword" (Matthew 26:52). Let me stress two points in connection with this passage. There is the insistence on "all." There is no distinction between a good and a bad use of the sword. The sheer fact of using the sword entails this result. The law of the sword is a total law. Then, Jesus is in no sense making a moral valuation or announcing a divine intervention or a coming judgment; he simply describes the reality of what is happening. He states one of the laws of violence. Violence creates violence, begets and procreates violence. The violence of the colonialists creates the violence of the anticolonialists, which in turn exceeds that of the colonialists. Nor does victory bring any kind of freedom. Always, the victorious side splits up into clans which perpetuate violence. The violence of the blacks at Newark was justified. But it prompted the violence of the forces of order, whose Commission of Inquiry declared (February 12, 1968) that the black riot was not justified. I find this commission very interesting. It stated clearly: ". . . our country cannot fulfill its promises when terror reigns in the streets and when disorder and disregard of the law tear our communities apart. . . . No group can improve its condition by revolt." Well and good. But to remedy the situation the commission recommends measures looking to centralized government control (which would only invite more federal interference and also infringe on the citizens' liberties); for example, development, on the federal level, of a plan for coping with disorder, and the creation of a special police force for sup-pressing riots. How can anyone fail to see that (people being what they are) this means a stronger system of repression—the normal result of violence. And as the violence of the government increases, the people, their own violence temporarily curbed, nurse their hatred. The French and the Italians were held in check by the Nazi occupation. The moment they were liberated, their violence exploded, and they perpetrated crimes and torturings that imitated the atrocities of the Germans. I am bound to say that I saw no difference at all between the Nazi concentration camps and the camps in which France confined the "collaborators" in 1944 (at Eysses or Mauzac, for example).

The man who, in whatever way, uses violence should realize that he is entering into a reciprocal kind of relation capable of being renewed indefinitely. The ethic of violence is a truly new ethic, permitting neither peace nor surcease. "Suppression" of a revolt is not intended to assure peace. In this respect, the Hitlerites were more honest than our modern socialists, anticolonialists, etc. They made no pretenses about wanting to usher in an era of peace. They said frankly that their aim was to establish a new ethic, a new norm of human relationships, namely, violence. No, they were not savage beasts; they were straight-thinking men who had made violence the supreme value in life, the thing that gave a meaning to life. What our moralists and theologians of violence take to be a new and recent discovery is simply the result, and at the same time a repercussion, of what the Hitlerites proclaimed. We have not escaped the Nazi contamination of violence; and in their ways of operating, the anticolonialist movements still echo Nazism. Violence imprisons its practitioners in a circle that cannot be broken by human means. Study of the possible results of violence shows that it will have only one certain result: the reciprocity and the reproduction of violence. Whether any other results are attained—equal rights, legitimate defense, liberation, etc. —is wholly a matter of chance, and all those results, too, are subject to the reciprocity which is one of the laws of violence.

The third law of violence is sameness. Here I shall only say that it is impossible to distinguish between justified and unjustified violence, between violence that liberates and violence that enslaves. (We shall return to this problem farther on.) Every violence is identical with every other violence. I maintain that all kinds of violence are the same. And this is true not only of physical violence—the violence of the soldier who kills, the policeman who bludgeons, the rebel who commits arson, the revolutionary who assassinates; it is true also of economic violence—the violence of the privileged proprietor against his workers, of the "haves" against the "have-nots"; the violence done in international economic relations between our own societies and those of the Third World; the violence done through powerful corporations which exploit the resources of a country that is unable to defend itself. Examples of this last are oil in the Middle East, or the agricultural specialization (cotton, sugarcane, bananas, etc.) forced on a country that is totally the victim of exploitation. Asturias has demonstrated that, even though no shot is fired, sheer violence is at work.

Psychological violence also is subject to the law of sameness. It is simply violence, whether it takes the form of propaganda, biased reports, meetings of secret societies that inflate the egos of their members, brainwashing, or intellectual terrorism. In all these cases the victim is subjected to violence and is led to do what he did not want to do, so that his capacity for further personal development is destroyed. Psychological violence, though it seems less cruel than the policemen's bludgeon, is in fact worse, because the reaction it stimulates does not take the form of pride or self-assertion.

The psychological violence all countries employ is absolutely the worst of violences, because it lays hold of the whole man, and, without his knowing it, gelds him. Violence means all these things, and to try to differentiate among them is to evade the problem. The velvet-glove violence of the powerful who maintain the regimes of injustice, exploitation, profiteering, and hatred has its exact counterpart in the iron-fist violence of the oppressed. Likewise the violence of nations, be they weak or powerful, encourages violence in their people. When a nation—as all European nations do—trains its young men in the most extreme kinds of violence in order to prepare them for battle (parachutists, etc.), the result is bound to be that the whole nation imitates this violence.

Moreover, to say that sameness is one of the laws of violence is to say that, on the one hand, violence has no limits and, on the other, that condoning violence means condoning every kind of violence. Once you choose the way of violence, it is impossible to say, "So far and no further"; for you provoke the victim of your violence to use violence in turn, and that necessarily means using greater violence. We have seen the so-called escalation of war in Vietnam. But, mind, this "escalation" is not a result of chance or of a government's wickedness; there never are limits to violence. When you begin to employ torture in order to get information, you cannot say: "This bit of torturing is legitimate and not too serious, but I'll go no further." The man who starts torturing necessarily goes to the limit; for if he decides to torture in order to get information, that information is very important; and if, having used a "reasonable" kind of torture, he does not get the information he wants, what then? He will use worse torture. The very nature of violence is such that it has no limits. We have seen that it is impossible to set up laws of warfare. Either no war happens to be going on, and then it is easy to make agreements as to the limitations that should be established; or else a war is under way, and then all agreements fall before the imperative of victory.

Violence is hubris, fury, madness. There are no such things as major and minor violence. Violence is a single thing, and it is always the same. In this respect, too, Jesus saw the reality. He declared that there is no difference between murdering a fellow man and being angry with him or insulting him (Matthew 5:21-22). This passage is no "evangelical counsel for the converted"; it is, purely and simply, a description of the nature of violence.

Now the third aspect of this sameness that characterizes violence: once we consent to use violence ourselves, we have to consent to our adversary's using it, too. We cannot demand to receive treatment different from that we mete out. We must understand that our own violence necessarily justifies the enemy's, and we cannot object to his violence. This is true in two senses. A government that maintains itself in power only by violence (economic, psychological, physical, or military violence, or just plain violence) absolutely cannot protest when guerrillas, revolutionaries, rioters, criminals attack it violently. It cannot plead that it represents justice legitimately constraining dangerous assassins. And this holds even when economic violence is met by physical violence. But the opposite also holds, namely, that the revolutionary or the rioter cannot protest when the government uses violence against him. To condone revolutionary violence is to condone the state's violence. Yet in recent years we have been hearing endless protests from the revolutionaries. They seem to think that all the "rights" are on their side, but that the state may act only in strict accordance with the law. Almost every week rioters complain about police brutality; what about their own brutality?

During the Algerian war, France's left-wing intellectuals constantly protested against the brutality of the French army and its use of torture, but pronounced legitimate the torturings and massacres committed by the National Liberation Front. "They have to do these things," we were told, "for no other way of operating is open to them." This "they have to" amounts to saying, "In the face of the increase of crime, we simply have to use torture as a preventive measure." The revolutionaries who claim for themselves the right to use violence but deny it to the state, who demand that the state act correctly, in the light of love, justice, and the common weal, are guilty of hypocrisy (such as Mr. Debray exhibited during his trial). I certainly do not condone the dictatorial government of a Barrientos. I do ask, however, that the man who uses violence at least have the courage to admit the consequences of his action, namely, violence against himself. Let him refrain from appealing to great principles—a Declaration of Rights, democracy, justice—in the hope of escaping the reaction of the power he has attacked. We must recognize, and clearly, that violence begets violence. Does anyone ask, "Who started it?" That is a false question. Since the days of Cain, there has been no beginning of violence, only a continuous process of retaliation. It is childish to suppose that today's conditions are unprecedented, to say, "There are dangerous communists about, we must be on guard against them," or, "This government is basely imperialistic and dictatorial, we must overthrow it." When a man is born, violence is already there, already present in him and around him.

Violence begets violence—*nothing else*. This is the fourth law of violence. Violence is par excellence the method of falsehood. "We have in view admirable ends and objectives. Unfortunately, to attain them we have to use a bit of violence. But once we are the government, you will see how society develops, how the living standard rises and cultural values improve. If we revolutionaries are only allowed to use a little violence (you can't make an omelet without breaking eggs), you'll see the reign of justice, liberty, and equality." That kind of thing is repeated again and again, and it sounds logical enough. But it is a lie. I am not making a moral judgment here, but a factual experimental judgment based on experience. Whenever a violent movement has seized power, it has made violence the law of power. The only thing that has changed is the person who exercises violence. No government established by violence has given the people either liberty or justice—only a show of liberty (for those who supported the movement) and a show of justice (which consists in plundering the erstwhile "haves"). And I am speaking not only of the revolutions of 1789, 1917, or 1933, or the revolutions of Mao, Nasser, Ben Bella, Castro; what I say above is true also of "liberal" or "democratic" governments (I have cited the U.S.A. as an example). Sometimes indeed such a government is captured by the very thing it fights. To combat communist propaganda by "good propaganda" is in fact to fall victim to the psychological violence of the enemy. The violent struggle against racism —at first against Hitler's racism—has caused the development of racism throughout the world. Before 1935, racism was very rare and sporadic. But the opposition to Hitler's racism, by propaganda and by arms, made the opposers familiar with his vision of man and society. In fighting racism by violence we have all become racists.* In the United

---

* Characteristically, Pastor Albert B. Cleage, Jr., of Detroit, one of the leading spokesmen for black power in the U.S.A., declared that violence is *redemptive*. (The idea of violence as purificatory was advanced in France to justify the violence of the liberation in 1944-45.) But after the riots Pastor Cleage said: "Now we are no longer afraid; now it is the white man who is afraid." Quite right. But this proves that violence is not redemptive and that, contrary to Pastor Cleage's opinion, violence does not open the way to negotiation but only transfers fear from one side to the other.

States, the moment the struggle became violent, the blacks began to move from antiracism to racism. Exactly the same thing happened in the case of anticolonialism: its corollary, evident among all the African peoples, is nationalism. And the spirit of nationalism cannot be expressed save by violence. The French resistance to Nazism aimed to create a free and just republic. In 1945, the *same resisters* massacred 45,000 people at Sétif in Algeria, and in 1947 they massacred almost 100,000 in Madagascar.

It is a very serious matter that in spite of multiplied experiences, every one of which showed that violence begets violence, there should still be illusions on this score. Violence can never realize a noble aim, can never create liberty or justice. I repeat once more that the end does not justify the means, that, on the contrary, evil means corrupt good ends. But I repeat also: "Let the man who wants to use violence, do so; let the man who thinks there is no other way, use it; but let him know what he is doing." That is all the Christian can ask of this man—that he be aware that violence will never establish a just society. Yes, he will get his revenge; yes, he will subdue his "enemy"; yes, he will consummate his hatred. But let him not confuse hate with justice. I quote from J. Lasserre's article "Révolution et non-violence": *
"We do not believe that peace can come out of violence, that justice can issue from generalized criminality, that respect for man can emerge from contemptuousness. Hatred and crime result neither in justice nor in reconciliation, but in bitterness, cowardice, vice and crime. . . . All these attitudes are in no way propitious for the creation of a just and humane society. . . . [Those who hold them] have bent the knee to the bloody idol. And since they are swept along by the internal logic of violence, their struggle soon ceases

* *Cahiers de la réconciliation*, Paris, 1967, pp. 34–36.

to be a means of attaining justice and becomes an end in it-self. Ultimately, the cruelest and most clamorous among them take over—the toughest, not the most just. And the revolution is aborted under the dictatorship of a new tyrant. How can you defend and build man when you begin by sup-pressing and destroying men?" In other words—words that apply to absolutely all cases: "Violence never attains the ob-jectives it sets up." And, tragically, the proponents of vio-lence always talk the same way. Here are some sentences that appeared in *Le Monde* (April 27, 1967):

"What a wonderful future we could look forward to, and soon, if only two or three or more Vietnams flourished [*sic*] on the surface of the globe, each with its countless dead, its terrible tragedies and its daily feats of heroism, each delivering blow after blow to imperialism, compelling it to spread its forces thin to meet the assault of the growing hatred of the world's peoples! . . . Where we die does not matter much. Death will be welcome, if only our war cry penetrates receptive ears, if only another hand reaches out to take our weapons, if only other men rise up to intone the funeral chants as the machine guns crackle and new battle cries and songs of victory sound out."

Who said that—Hitler or Che Guevara? No one could tell, save for the fact that Vietnam is mentioned. (Hitler too often attacked imperialism.) But who could imagine that a leader capable of such words would lead the way to justice and freedom?

Finally, the fifth law of violence is this: the man who uses violence always tries to justify both it and himself. Violence is so unappealing that every user of it has produced lengthy apologies to demonstrate to the people that it is just and mor-ally warranted. Hitler, Stalin, Mao, Castro, Nasser, the guer-rillas, the French "paras" of the Algerian war—all tried to vindicate themselves. The plain fact is that violence is never "pure." Always violence and hatred go together. I spoke above of the rather useless piece of advice once given Christians: that they should make war without hatred. Today it is utterly clear that violence is an expression of hatred, has its source in hatred and signifies hatred. And only a completely heartless person would be capable of simply affirming hatred, without trying to exonerate himself. Those who exalt violence—a Stokely Carmichael or a Rap Brown, for instance—connect it directly with hatred. Thus Rap Brown declared: "Hate has a role to play. I am full of hatred, and so are the other blacks. Hate, like violence, is necessary for our revolution." Carmichael has repeatedly spoken of the close relation between hate and violence. In one of his speeches* he declared: "As Che Guevara said, we must develop hatred in order to transform man into a machine for killing."

It is absolutely essential for us to realize that there is an unbreakable link between violence and hatred. Far too often intellectuals, especially, imagine that there is a sort of pure, bloodless violence, an abstract violence, like that of Robespierre, who dispassionately ordered executions. We must understand that, on the contrary, hatred is the motivator of violence. If I quote Brown and Carmichael it is not because they have a monopoly on hatred, but rather because they state, boldly and clearly, the truth that is universally relevant. A government, when it goes to war, can afford to refrain from declarations and proclamations of hatred of the enemy (unless Hitler is the enemy!), because, being in a position of power, it can put on a show of magnanimity. Nevertheless, the violence exercised by the French and American governments in Algeria and Vietnam, respectively,

* At the conference in Havana, August 2, 1967.

involves hatred, only in these cases the hatred is expressed by intermediaries. The head of the government can keep on declaring his good will, his objectivity, his freedom from hate, for he is not directly engaged in the military action. He can keep on pretending to pray and professing to love humanity. He can praise nonviolence, as President Johnson did when Martin Luther King was assassinated. But all that is façade. A ruler has to save face and show that he is a well-disposed man; he has to justify himself! But this means becoming part of the system characteristic of violence, which tries to justify itself. Brown and Carmichael also follow this pattern, and even while they justify themselves they continue to protest their blamelessness. Listen to Brown: "The white taught us violence. Violence is a part of American culture. . . . The only answer to slaughter is slaughter. . . . We hate the white because he has always hated us. . . . A black cannot love himself unless he hates the white." *
And Carmichael: "The white exploits people, he must be crushed. . . . Violence is the only way to destroy the American capitalism that oppresses us." † Usually, history or the need to retaliate or the unavailability of other means is cited to justify violence. The argument runs: (1) Violence is inherent in history, history makes for violence (an argument we shall deal with further on); or (2) "We are treated with violence, and the only way to cope with that is violence" (which is a confirmation—and out of the mouth of the proponents of violence—of what I have called a law of violence, namely, continuity. But these apologists forget that their own violence also creates new violence!); or (3) "Such

---

* In an interview published in the *Nouvel observateur*, September, 1967.
† *Ibid.* I certainly agree that the colonialists and the whites started the violence. But here I am stressing only one point, namely, the system of justification.

and such a system is unjust, and only violence can change it. We are driven to violence."

Very often, purely imaginary constructs are set up to excuse, sustain, or justify hatred. Countless writings show this concern for legitimacy. But it soon becomes plain that if you are going to justify your violence, it cannot be just any kind of violence. There has to be a legitimate kind of violence! Thus, for example, Father Jarlot stated:* "Unjust violence can be repelled only by just violence." And he called for a theology of just violence. But how could he miss seeing that, in saying this, he was entering into the vicious circle that "just war" theologians were caught in and have never escaped from; they have emitted only platitudes and empty phrases. And to pose the problem of just violence is to start that whole thing over again. What makes violence just? Its objective? We have seen that violence corrupts the best of ends. Is it the way it is used that makes violence just? But violence has no limits. Here is sheer stupidity. Stokely Carmichael recently declared that the blacks do not want to fight in Vietnam. "We don't want to be a generation of murderers," he said (and that meant: we don't want to go to Vietnam to fight). "To escape that, we are ready to plunge the United States into chaos." † This means that using violence to create chaos in the United States is right, but fighting in Vietnam is murdering. This is a very common type of "reasoning." It shows up the weakness of the pro-violence position; for this position is based entirely on irrational choices and blind hatred. But there is the need to feel justified! And at that point violence can be quite as hypocritical as the conservative bourgeois system. Hitler's system is the best example in point.

* At a press conference held at the Vatican, March 26, 1968, on the occasion of the anniversary of the encyclical *Populorum progressio.*

† Discours à la mutualité, Paris, December 6, 1967.

The violence of the Hitler party in 1932 and 1933 was fascinating to watch. Cynical in the face of bourgeois hypocrisy, it aimed to destoy the traditional moral system and to create a virile community; to repudiate paternalism, exalt stern self-control and willingness to meet death, and establish equality at whatever cost in pain and suffering. All this was an ideal that, to the young athirst for absolutes, seemed far nobler than the mediocre aims proposed by those of their countrymen who frankly favored violence. But this ideal was mere verbiage, façade; this was "pure" violence. What came of it was an orthodoxy, a statism, more rigorous and coercive than the one it displaced; a morality just as hypocritical as the old one, a social conformism just as blind, and a dictatorship that fooled the people with its lies.

Violence is hypocritical. And to say that the question of legitimizing violence is a false question is also hypocritical. For to say that is to say in effect that violence can be legitimized only by "the communal action of men, which is a revolutionary action."* But if any action, provided it be the "communal action of men," legitimizes violence, then we shall have to put up with a great many wars fought by enthusiasts who completely disregard the authorities. And to say that revolutionary action itself legitimizes violence is to introduce a value judgment. People do not start a revolution blindly, without cause and without hope of success. First, they decide that the conditions obtaining are bad, and then . . . So, like it or not, all this leads back to a theory of just violence!

It is very important to be clear about this persistent longing for justification. I do not say that the practitioner of violence feels uneasy and that therefore he must be experiencing pangs of conscience; but in acting violently he is so

---

* Abribat at the Bordeaux conference, February 15, 1967.

unsure of himself that he has to have an ideological construct that will put him at ease intellectually and morally. That is why the person inclined to violence is necessarily the victim propaganda aims at; and, conversely, violence is the theme that above all others lends itself to propaganda. Champions of violence ought to do a little thinking about the poor moral quality of those who are led to violence, and also about the fact that there can be no political violence without propaganda—that is, without engineering demonstrations, without debasing man even as it professes to liberate and exalt him. *

These are the laws of violence, unchanging and inescapable. We must understand them clearly if we are to know what we are doing when we damn violence.

ARE THERE TWO KINDS OF VIOLENCE?

Finally, we must examine a view that is very often advanced—the view, namely, that there are two totally different kinds of violence. While the Algerian war was going on, Casalis, the professor of theology, declared: "There is a violence that liberates and a violence that enslaves." This statement can be taken as summarizing the position of many intellectuals (Duverger, Domenach, etc.). To illustrate: During the Algerian war, the National Liberation Front used violence to liberate the people from the French colonial yoke; therefore, while violence must be condemned, this particular violence was to be condoned. But the French army used violence to keep the people enslaved, thus adding servitude to violence.

Duverger explains that violence may fall in with the trend of history. He takes up the well-known idea of revolution as

---

* On the relation between violence, justification, and propaganda, see my *Propaganda* (New York: Knopf, 1965).

the midwife of history. And so far as it accords with the trend of history, violence as means must be condoned. Thus communist violence is in line with history, but fascist, capitalist, or colonialist violence must be condemned because it goes counter to the trend of history. Likewise Father Jarlot, who declares: "There are structures that are unjust in themselves, because they are serious obstacles to realization of the legitimate aspirations of millions of people and to the necessary social and economic development of their country."* Here the distinction between the two kinds of violence is based on what is held to be the need of "unglueing" economics and society (in "stages," as laid down by W. W. Rostov). Father Régamey makes the same distinction, but in more classic fashion: "The violence that is an unjust aggression, from outside, against persons, is bad violence, even though this injustice be called order. The violence that is a last resort— there truly being no other way to achieve the genuine good of persons—is good violence." † However, Father Régamey adds honestly: "The distinction between good and bad violence is quite clear in theory, but applying it is terribly puzzling." Puzzling indeed! Moreover, if we are to take his words seriously we must first know what the injustice is that he makes his criterion. The same strictures apply to Father Jarlot's statements.

But "the genuine good of persons" seems to me even more puzzling. In the first place, what is that "genuine good" of persons? Their standard of living, their physical well-being, their participation in political life, their personal development, or perhaps their "eternal salvation"? And, finally, Father Régamey's appeal to "persons" leaves me even more in doubt, for he carefully ignores the persons who are the vic-

* *Loc. cit.*
† *Op. cit.*, p. 27.

tims of this just violence. No one can convince me that the expulsion of the French settlers from Algeria was for their good (even if the reason for their expulsion was their own violence in the past), or that the murder and torture of Battista's partisans was for their good. The unhappy fact is that violence operates only for the good of its users.

Others are insisting these days that, in a class-ridden society, violence is the only possible relation between the classes. So the oppressed class, which bodies forth the future, may validly use violence, but the other class may not. To say this, however, is not merely to set up a moral criterion for violence; it is to assert that there are two kinds of violence which have nothing in common, indeed are not of *the same nature*. This line of thought is developed further. Some say that one cannot speak about the state as such, that everything depends on the end the state is pursuing. If that end is socialism, for example, the state is legitimate. But this notion leaves out of account the fact that, by its very structure, the modern state controls socialism and perverts it, turning it into nonsocialism. Others declare that nationalism is a fine thing when it leads to the liberation of peoples; it is only Europe's old-fashioned nationalism that they condemn. But this is to close one's eyes to the fact that the characteristics of nationalism are always the same, that a young, liberating nationalism has exactly the same sociological structure as German or French nationalism, and that the transition from "young" to "old" nationalism is tragically swift. China and Algeria are examples of how, in the course of a few years, a young nationalism turns into an old, sclerotic nationalism.

But to return to violence. I remind my readers that we are trying to apply the realism that is inherent in the Christian faith, trying to look at reality without being misled by words. Let us then ask what, concretely, is the result, the actual result of "legitimate, liberating" violence. It is plain that in every case this violence has in fact led to establishing a greater violence. Well then, if violence is a continuous process, where does it end? This is the first question we must ask. What did Algeria's National Liberation Front achieve by its use of violence? Elimination of the French, of course; but also an economic recession, the establishment of a dictatorial state, a false and altogether regressive socialism, and the condemnation of all who had participated in the violent struggle, because they proved completely unfitted for conducting a rational government. In what way does it move with the tide of history? So we must try to determine whither violence is leading. And this is one of the insurmountable obstacles that make a mockery of the theory of just violence.

Domenach writes that violence must be condoned as a means of combating social injustice or of coping with the violence of others—provided, however, that it be used for the benefit of others, not for that of its practitioner. This requires an impossible casuistry. We would have to be able to measure out exactly the amount of violence needed to achieve the result aimed at. But we have seen that the result aimed at is purely ideological and *never* coincides with the result achieved by the use of violence. We have seen, too, that violence by its very nature is without limits—that there is no such thing as a tiny dose of violence for realizing this or that particular purpose. Let us do some computing. The evil I want to inflict on the other (who is bad, either because of his personal qualities or because he belongs to a certain race, class, or nation or holds certain opinions)—is the evil I inflict justified by the evil he has done? I am not asking for a moral or spiritual judgment but for a realistic one. Is there any justification? At the very least, my violence must not be worse and more far-reaching than his. How am I to know this? If you protest, "I am only defending myself,"

I have no more to say; but then we are at the animal level. How else can I measure the quantity of violence? Is torturing with a razor, as the National Liberation Front did, worse or less bad than torturing with electricity, as the French paras did?

Further, I would have to consider the number of people involved. Take the case of a minority oppressing a majority (the bourgeoisie oppressing the proletariat or a colonialist nation oppressing a colonized people). Their suffering justifies the majority in using violence against the oppressive minority. But what if the situation is reversed? What if the minority is crushed by the majority? Is violence legitimate in this case because the largest group uses it against the smallest? Was the Bolshevik dictatorship's suppression of the kulaks better than what obtained under the tsarist regime? Was Ho Chi Minh's torture, execution, spoliation, and banishment of the Vietnamese Catholics—a minority, though four million strong—more acceptable than the action of the French in protecting the Catholics and oppressing the Indo-Chinese people? Who will make this calculation? Who will gauge the gravity of violence against a single person? Looking at the situation concretely shows that the evil arising from violence will never be neatly calculable. The one thing that is true in this connection is that, on the moral scale, violence exercised against a single human being is an absolute weight, whatever the form, the result or the cause of that violence. And there really is no difference between the violence done one person and the violence done a million persons. As to the reference to history, that is a lie.

Now, concerning my strictures on Algeria, I shall be told, "But wait for the outcome. When Algeria has recovered its equilibrium, when it realizes socialism . . ." I answer: Who will see the outcome? How many generations will it take to realize socialism—and what kind of socialism? Absolutely nothing that is happening there today gives even the smallest assurance that Algeria is moving ahead toward "socialism." Well then, what element in all this justifies the violence that is going on today? In what direction is current history moving?

In short, the idea that there are two kinds of violence is utterly mistaken. From whatever side the problem is approached, it invariably turns out that all violence is of a piece, that it follows the laws formulated above. That is why it can be affirmed that violence never attains the objectives it announces as justifying its use. The objectives and ends it proclaims always relate to man—to man's existence, condition, and destiny. Indeed the champions of violence present their case humanistically, so to speak. According to them, violence is legitimized by being put into the service of man. They never call for violence in defense of an institution or an abstract value. When these are invoked it is purely as a matter of form. But it is obvious that, on the concrete level, institutional reforms never satisfy the proponents of violence, even if they demanded those reforms. For violence must go ever further.

Here is an important point: On the level of institutions or values, it is possible to distinguish between end and means. On this level only, the traditional distinction holds up. Institutions exist only for and through men. But while institutions are always the creation of human beings, and whether they are just or unjust, effectual or ineffectual depends entirely on the people who use them. Values have no meaning except as they are lived by man! We always come back to man. Everything depends on how man relates to man. But violence always breaks and corrupts the relation of men to each other. And I am not impressed if someone says, "But violence has already broken and corrupted that relation."

That is no reason for those who claim to represent justice to continue violence. We Europeans know all too well that colonialist violence has torn apart every human relationship; and alas, we know that we are to blame. The writings of Albert Camus, or Montherlant's *Rose des Sables,* witnessed to Europe's guilt long before Frantz Fanon, justifiably, raised his angry cry. Again, it is a fact that our university professors have never had a truly human relationship with their students. It is a fact that by degrading the colonialist peoples the colonialist corrupted humanity, and that by making his students into show animals the professor also corrupted humanity.

But we have a right to say: "If you protest against this degradation and this corruption, do better. Re-establish an authentic and true relationship among men, restore nobility to man. But you won't do that by humiliating, torturing, or degrading the colonialist, the bourgeois, or the professor. Your violence also kills man's authenticity. The system you want to set up also corrupts. You, too, break the relationship of man to man—and among yourselves as well as outside your ranks. For violence—your just violence!—is contagious. You use violence against the enemy. In time, violence will be used against you!"

However, institutions established through "just" violence are never an improvement. Just violence envisions human relationships of a particular kind, and these cannot be realized without coercive institutions. These institutions will not establish freedom, because they are violent. They cannot be free institutions unless all the opposing parties reach an agreement—unless there is not one person left who seeks revenge, not one person who sees the institution as a powerful machine that rides roughshod over him. Similarly, liberating violence cannot establish a society's values; for if they are to be communal values they will have to be accepted as good and true by every member of the community (not only by a majority). But that can never happen when the values are imposed by, or as the result of, violence. Whatever his own faults, the victim will never recognize those values. Obviously, the murderer does not recognize the policeman's values. The Algerian war certainly has not led the Algerians to accept Western values—though the Castro and Nasser dictatorships are certainly no advertisement for socialist values. Here the problem of means corrupting ends comes up again, indirectly. Violence has long-lasting effects on the man who suffers it. It cannot be said that the effects of violence end when violence ends. The victim carries the effect on his body and in his heart and subconscious for years, perhaps all the rest of his life.

People who talk about "just violence" ought to know all this. To support their assertion that there are two kinds of violence, they would have to do what in fact they often do: refuse to recognize reality; namely, the law of violence. That is why I consider it so very important to point out that a realistic attitude is basic to a true understanding of the phenomenon of violence. But this implies rejection of idealisms.

REJECTION OF IDEALISMS

Invariably, an idealism serves to justify the use of violence —the idealism that consists in taking violence for something other than it is. This idealism is of a piece with that (described earlier in this book) which sees the violence exercised by a government not as such but as "public force." Even those who are strongly in favor of violence resort to this idealism. They throw a veil of political, economic, or philosophical considerations around violence, or they create what amounts to a mythology of violence, exalting it into a kind of value (as Sorel does). Certainly when you collide with a value no blood will flow. The mystical exaltation of violence at the hands of Hitler and of all modern revolu-tionaries makes people forget that violence means blood-shed, means human beings screaming in pain and fear. Let us briefly consider the various aspects of this idealism.

The type of idealism most widespread today is revolu-tionary idealism. Intellectuals especially are prone to it. How many French professors of philosophy glorify Che Guevara and make extremely violent speeches. Malraux had an an-swer for them: "If you really believe that the welfare of humanity depends on the guerrillas you will go to Bolivia to help them fight; otherwise, you had best keep silent on this subject."*

The usual themes of revolutionary idealism are two: vio-lence as liberating and violence as purificatory. The person who is crushed in our society, who feels profoundly at odds with it and wants to challenge it radically—this person talks about violence and sometimes practices it. For violence is a way of escaping from conformism, of breaking with the bourgeois environment and rejecting compromise. Violence, the revolutionary declares, reveals the facts, strips the mask from social hypocrisy, exposes the true condition of human-ity to the light of day, and so divides society that its tradi-tional ways of acting, its morals and organization can no longer stand up. Violence is beneficial surgery; it cauterizes the flesh to kill the poison; it purifies both itself and society. Violence liberates man from the false rules imposed on him by society, from the wearying grind of daily toil. It leads him into an adventure through which he may become a

---

* Interview with Malraux, *Europe No. 1*, October 27, 1967.

complete man. I could write pages about this hypostasis of violence. Today, in exact imitation of Hitler, the partisans of the guerrillas idealize violence in this fashion. But this idealism also throws a veil over violence and insists that there is no violence when in fact violence obtains everywhere. Robespierre and St. Juste showed the way when they declared that the Reign of Terror during the French revolution was a form of government required by the circumstances and therefore entirely legitimate. Since then all governments have hidden their violence under a mask of legality. It was Karl Marx's great merit that he brought into the open certain facts: the proprietor's domination of the worker is violence, even if it involves no act of cruelty; class war goes on even if the proprietor does not call for police or army intervention; an army serves first and foremost as guarantor of the power of the ruling class. But all this is disguised by legal fictions, political doctrines, and appeals to patriotism. The Christian must tear away this hypocritical, idealistic mask and at the same time must condemn the idealism that interprets violence as purificatory and sanctifying.

Moreover, violence is always used in the conviction that it is the only means adequate for attaining a noble end—social justice, the nation's welfare, elimination of criminals (for the political or social enemy is always considered a criminal), radical change of the economic structures. Those who propose just revolution always represent violence as the "point of no return," with which, consequently, history is obliged to come to terms. But my study of politics and sociology has convinced me that violence is an altogether superficial thing; that is, it can produce apparent, superficial changes, rough facsimiles of change. But it never affects the roots of injustice—social structures, the bases of an economic system, the foundations of a society. Violence is not the means appropriate for a revolution "in depth." * It succeeds in eliminating a group of directors, of resented neighbors, embarrassing witnesses, hated oppressors, but it never creates decisive change. A new police force, a new factory manager replace the old ones. Thus the belief that violence can effect decisive change arises from a dangerous idealism that promotes violence and produces illusions of the worst kind.

Another idealism we must reject is what I shall call "generous" idealism. This wears many forms. For instance, it proclaims that the great desideratum is reconciliation, and that, once violence has done its work, reconciliation will be possible at last. This is a Marxian vision of a paradise where man will be reconciled with himself, with his fellow men, with nature; but the necessary preliminary to this paradise is bloody contention and the dictatorship of the proletariat. Some Christians sympathize with this idea. T. Richard Snyder, for instance, suggests that the Christian preachment of reconciliation is unrealistic because it does not take account of the violence that is a necessary preliminary.†

Then there is the generous idealism of so many young men who risk imprisonment or death rather than participate in a war they condemn only because they idealize and whitewash their country's enemy. Those young men are heroes and fools both. They are repelled by the violence they see— the massive, enormous violence that cries to heaven. And here they are right. But seeing this highly visible violence, they forthwith make lambs, saints, and martyrs of its victims. For they close their eyes to what the enemy is really

* These statements are developed in a study of revolution that I am presently engaged in writing.

† In his review of the Fanon and Debray volumes, in *The Christian Century*, January 17, 1968.

like, to his cruelty, his violence, his lies. They overlook his real intentions; they overlook the fact that he would use terrible violence if he won power. Poor young men, totally unknowing, uncomprehending, blind, perceiving only what is happening now! So they side with the enemy and countenance the enemy's violence.

In France, before the Second World War, a great many people sided with the Nazis. Hadn't the Nazis, out of their generosity, protested against the violence done the Sudeten Germans, the Croats, the Germans of Danzig? Hadn't they declared that they would defend the rights of the poor and the unemployed, the victims exploited by the capitalists? Their admiration of the Nazis cost those people dearly. Again, after the war, many French people sided with communism, "the party of the poor, the proletariat." A few years later they were stunned by the declarations of the Twentieth Communist Congress and by Moscow's suppression of the Hungarian revolt. This is the kind of idealism that must be combated and radically condemned.

But there is also a pacifist idealism, and this is especially suspect. I can hardly omit mentioning the hippies in this connection. They, too, have been generous-minded. There is, of course, the matter of drugs and sexual freedom, but this has not been the most important thing about the hippies. They have been opposed to society as a whole, and with good reason. They repudiate society because of its conformism, its moral emptiness, its loss of soul. They proclaim Flower Power—perhaps in opposition to Black Power, certainly in opposition to all forms of violence. They predict the end of the West—and they are at least partly right, for the only ideal the West cherishes is economic growth. Their appeal to love, their partial adoption of the thought of Krishna, their repudiation of nationalism in favor of a sense of common humanity and universal understanding, are all laudable. And their appeal to the individual to exercise his initiative so that he may discover what "his thing" is and help to shape a new nonmoralistic ethic suggests what true ethical Christian preaching might be. All this is truly valid and profoundly serious, however debatable the external aspects of hippie-dom may be. We ought to join in their insistence on non-violence as the absolute principle, in their condemnation of all forms of violence.

Unfortunately, all this splendid élan seems doomed from the start, because the hippies have no understanding of what their real place in society is. What I censure in them is not their vice or their contentiousness, but their complete lack of realism. (Of course, as we all know, they will say that they do not want to be realists, for to be so would mean acquiesc-ing in the very things they reject in our rationalistic civi-lization.) They do not know that the reality of this society—a violent society, devoted to technology and to production-consumption—is the basis of their own existence. They are a supplement to this same society—the flower on its hat, its song, its garland, its fireworks display, its champagne cork. They reject and indict it—so they think. In reality, they are only the product of its luxuriousness. They cannot exist ma-terially unless this society functions fully. For insofar as they work little or not at all, yet consume a not inconsiderable amount of goods (even if they refuse to use machines), they are an unproductive load on that society. Only a society that has reached a certain level of production and consumption can support a few of its members in idleness. The hippies are in fact a product of the luxury that a highly productive so-ciety can afford. Obviously, the hippie movement could not exist in a poorer society or in one experiencing a period of limited growth, simply because, in such societies, all the young people would be regimented and forced to work hard,

or perhaps would starve to death. But if they live in a rich society, they depend in fact on the existence of those economic mechanisms, technical rigors, and open or hidden
violences that form the warp of that society. Were it not for
that society's morality of high returns, exploitation, competition, and "progress" (though "progress," the hippies
rightly object, is a misnomer), they simply could not exist
at all.

Yet, on the other hand, the hippies seem to be the answer
to a deep need experienced by that same society. Such a society is subject to boredom. Unconsciously, it senses its own
lack of youth and enjoyment. Gloomy, dull, and joyless, it
thinks of itself neither as representing the utmost in good living nor as a paradise. It is always on the prowl, trying to discover what it is that is wanting. Such a society provides lei-
sure and distractions, but these are not enough; you have to
know how to use them! The members of such a society are
not happy, do not feel that they are free or better than others. They need a supplement (in addition to what they have,
of course!); and suddenly, there is the hippie, the perfect answer to their need. Need finds a way. The hippies introduce
color, youth, pleasure. To be sure, they are a bit shocking,
but a society held together by boredom is more or less proof
against shock. The important point in all this is that the hippie phenomenon, far from attacking this society, meets its
need, gives it what it lacked, what it must have if it is to remain what it is. For the hippies bring the complement of joy
to this rationalized, producing society, and so it can go on to
even better developments. The hippies' mistake is that they
think they are outside that society, when in fact they are its
origin and its product.

Their nonviolence is an idealism for several reasons. First,
they can exist as a nonviolent group only thanks to the order
and productiveness (which is to say, the violence) of that

society. Second, they think that, being themselves a society or a worldwide group, they can live in freedom and without violence; whereas they can live so only because they are surrounded by the *rest* of the society into which they have inserted themselves. Their Rousseauism cannot work except as the rest of society grows organizationally and develops more constraints. Sympathetic as I am to hippies, I fear that, because of their blindness as to both their true situation and significance and their relation to this world's society, they are in great danger of becoming a society of violence. Such a society always is organized under cover of the most generous idealism.

Finally, we must reject the kind of Christian idealism that appears from time to time in the history of the church. In one way or other, this idealism is always concerned with the goodness of the world of man. Christians find it most difficult to keep in mind the Bible's double affirmation of radical evil and radical love. For a while, they see only the radical evil of man and the world—and this means puritanism, moralism, emotional aridity, an end of forgiveness and joy. Or, again for a while, they see only grace and love, and then they think they are already in Paradise. Actually, the new theological orientations go in this direction. Their bases, as we are constantly reminded, are three in number. First, "God so loved the world . . ."; therefore the world actually *is* redeemed, is good. The work of salvation was undertaken for the world; therefore whatever happens in the world has already been blessed and loved by God. The work of this world is beneficial, and Christians ought to make their contribution to it. Second, where sin abounds, grace abounds more greatly. Of course, there is still evil in the world, but we ought not to concentrate on sin or be obsessed by it, for sin is totally within the system of grace, and grace is stronger than sin and all-encompassing. It is useless to analyze evils, disasters, economic or social corruption. Rather, remember that the operation of grace is evident in man's marvelous and excellent works, in his techniques, his politics, his science, etc.

Third, these idealists point to the Lordship of Jesus Christ over the world. If Jesus Christ is truly Lord, then all that happens in the world is under his Lordship. Therefore it is not in the church (with its rites and ceremonies and prayers) or even through study of the Bible that we participate in his Lordship, but in the world. It is by communion with all men (with men who know Christ and men who do not) that the kingdom of this Lord is built—this Lord who is present incognito in even the least of these (Matthew 25:40, 45).

These theological bases (they must, of course, be taken together, not singly) lead to putting a high value on man and the world, to exalting technological, scientific, and political works, and to defining the Christian's true vocation as participation in human culture. But systematically to make positive judgments of politics or technology leads to the rejection of all realism in regard to them and to a belief in progress. For example, consider that (as the Dominican priest Edward Schillebeeckx put it)* "the world as it is, is implicitly Christian," and that therefore all Christian participation in the world advances the Lord's work. For, curiously, where this theology formerly led to quietism, today it leads to activism. In the name of this theology (which is in part that of the World Council of Churches), Christians are induced to participate unreservedly and with a good conscience in political or scientific action; for, they are told, whatever evil

* At a conference in Brussels, March 13, 1968. Clearly, this statement is inspired by the theology of Pierre Teilhard de Chardin and his conception of "Holy Material."

there might be in such action will necessarily be overruled by the good.

Obviously, this idealism fosters illusions as to the reality of violence. On the one hand, Christian idealists are scandalized at the very possibility of violence. In their idyllic world, harshness, torture, and war seem abnormal and almost incomprehensible. But it is only gross, highly visible, undeniable violence that evokes this scandalized reaction. They deny the existence of masked, secret, covert violence—insofar as this can be concealed. (The violence of capitalist enterprise in the subject countries or the violence of Stalin's concentration camps was so well concealed that its existence could be denied.) But those Christian idealists fully approve the violence incidental to the revolt of the little people or the oppressed. They consider such violence an expression of justice. However, this approval is based on ignorance of what violence really is, on insufficient knowledge of the world, on blindness (voluntary or involuntary) to the results that violence always has, whatever the justification for it.

Yet the same Christians who so readily accept violence are incapable of killing a man themselves. Indeed they would probably be very much at a loss if someone handed them an automatic pistol.* But the theological error that underlies this idealization of violence leads them into a new, a sociopolitical Manicheanism which (like the earlier, metaphysical Manicheanism) is also an idealism, a simplifying re-

---

* An interesting example: Father Jaouen, who is famous in France for his work with the youth of Paris, declared that the film *Bonnie and Clyde* would not harm anyone; that the violence it showed was unimportant, that there was no danger of this film's making youth more violent. "For in France's society, there is no violence except that done by the police; and in the world, there is no violence except in Vietnam." (*Témoignage chrétien*, February 2, 1968). Surely blindness can be no blinder.

source to help people participate in a complicated world where, they know, they had better do what the powers that be recommend and take sides. So these Christians blindly take sides in an engagement that is in no way specifically Christian.

Thus, whatever its milieu, its motif, its basis or orientation, idealism always leads to the adoption of a false and dangerous position in regard to violence. The first duty of a Christian is to reject idealism.

4

The Fight of Faith

NECESSITY AND LEGITIMACY

As WE have just seen, Christian realism leads to the conclusion that violence is natural and normal to man and society, that violence is a kind of necessity imposed on governors and governed, on rich and poor. If this realism scandalizes Christians, it is because they make the great mistake of thinking that what is *natural* is *good* and what is *necessary* is *legitimate*. I am aware that the reader will answer at once: "You have shown that violence is inevitable and necessary in undertakings of any kind; *therefore* violence is legitimate, it *must* be used." This is anti-Christian reasoning par excellence. What Christ does for us is above all to make us free. Man becomes free through the Spirit of God, through conversion to and communion with the Lord. This is the one way to true freedom. But to have true freedom is to escape necessity or, rather, to be free to struggle against necessity. Therefore I say that only one line of action is open to the Christian who is free in Christ. He must struggle against violence precisely *because*, apart from Christ, violence is the form that human relations normally and necessarily take. In other words, the more completely violence seems to be of the order of necessity, the greater is the obligation of believers in Christ's Lordship to overcome it by challenging necessity.

This is the fixed, the immutable, and the radical basis of the Christian option in relation to violence. For the order of necessity is the order of separation from God. Adam, created by God and in communion with God, is free; he is not subject to any kind of necessity. God lays on him only one commandment, a commandment that is a word of God and therefore also both a gospel and an element in dialogue between persons. This commandment is not a law limiting his freedom from without. Adam knows nothing of necessity, obligation, inevitability. If he obeys the word, he does so freely. It is not at all necessary for him to labor, to *produce*, to defend the Garden against anyone. Necessity appears when Adam breaks his relation with God. Then he becomes subject to an order of obligation, the order of toil, hunger, passions, struggle against nature, etc., from which there is no appeal. At that moment necessity becomes part of the order of nature—not of nature as God wished it to be, but of nature henceforth made for death. And death is then the most total of all necessities. Necessity is definable as what man does because he cannot do otherwise. But when God reveals himself, necessity ceases to be destiny or even inevitability. In the Old Testament, man shatters the necessity of eating by fasting, the necessity of toil by keeping the Sabbath; and when he fasts or keeps the Sabbath he recovers his real freedom, because he has been found again by the God who has re-established communion with him. The institution of the order of Levites likewise shatters the normal institutional order of ownership, duty, provision for the future, etc. And this freedom is fully accomplished by and through Jesus Christ. For Christ, even death ceases to be a necessity: "I give my life for my sheep; it is not taken from me, I give it." And the constant stress on the importance of giving signifies a breaking away from the necessity of money.

Here then—all too briefly described—are the considerations basic to understanding the problem of violence. The temptation is always to yield to fatality, as Father Maillard does when he takes the extreme positions referred to above. "All life is a struggle," he says. "Life itself is violent. And it is in struggling that we realize ourselves. Every action is necessarily imperfect and impure. . . . We are caught in a terrible machine which can thrust us into situations of violence in spite of ourselves. Let us distrust the temptation to purity." * But Father Maillard confuses the situation he perceives so realistically with the will of God.

Violence is inevitable, but so far as concerns society it has the same character as the universally prevailing law of gravitation, which is not in any way an expression of God's love in Christ or of Christian vocation. When I stumble over an obstacle and fall, I am obeying the law of gravitation, which has nothing to do with Christian faith or the Christian life. We must realize that violence belongs to the same order of things. And so far as we understand that the *whole* of Christ's work is a work of liberation—of our liberation from sin, death, concupiscence, fatality (and from ourselves)— we shall see that violence is not simply an ethical option for us to take or leave. Either we accept the order of necessity, acquiesce in and obey it—and this has nothing at all to do with the work of God or obedience to God, however serious and compelling the reasons that move us—or else we accept the order of Christ; but then we must reject violence root and branch.

For the role of the Christian in society, in the midst of men, is to shatter fatalities and necessities. And he cannot fulfill this role by using violent means, simply because violence is of the order of necessity. To use violence is to be of the world. Every time the disciples wanted to use any kind

* *Cahiers de la réconciliation*, Paris, 1967.

of violence they came up against Christ's veto (the episode of the fire pouring from heaven on the cities that rejected Christ, the parable of the tares and the wheat, Peter's sword, etc.). This way of posing the problem is more radical than that implicit in the usual juxtaposition of violence and love. For as we shall see, there is a "violence of love," and there is necessarily a quarrel between "handless" love and effectual love. Naturally, there are those who will protest: "But can anyone say that he loves the exploited poor of South America when he does nothing for them; and can anything be done without violence?" On the contrary, there is no escaping the absolute opposition between the order of necessity and the order of Christ.

But now it must be evident why we had to begin by declaring the reality of violence, explaining that it is totally *of* the world, and showing in what ways it is a necessity. For the Christian, if he is to oppose violence, must recognize its full dimensions and its great importance. The better we understand that violence is necessary,* indispensable, inevitable, the better shall we be able to reject and oppose it. If we are free in Jesus Christ, we shall reject violence *precisely because* violence is necessary! We must say No to violence not *inasmuch* as it is a necessity and not only because it is violence. And, mind, this means *all* kinds and ways of violence: psychological manipulation, doctrinal terrorism, economic imperialism, the venomous warfare of free competition, as well as torture, guerrilla movements, police action. The capitalist who, operating from his headquarters, exploits the mass of workers or colonial peoples is just as violent as the guerrilla; he must absolutely not assume the mantle of Christianity. What he does is of the order of necessity, of estrangement from God; and even if he is a faith-

---

* Hitler said: "I cannot see why man should not be just as cruel as nature."

ful churchgoer and a highly educated man, there is no freedom in him.

But if this is true, the opposite is also true. Christians must
freely admit and accept the fact that non-Christians use violence. This is no reason for being scandalized. Just look at
the situation man is caught in—a hopeless situation from
which there is no escape. That is exactly what the order of
necessity is. The man who does not know freedom in Christ
cannot understand the word of freedom Paul spoke in the
midst of necessity: "We are afflicted in every way, but not
crushed; perplexed, but not driven to despair; persecuted,
but not forsaken; struck down, but not destroyed" (II Corinthians 4:8-9). Such a man thinks that in this situation
Paul should have used other means—violence in particular. We must accept and try to understand this man who
does not know Christ's freedom. But let us distinguish
clearly between him and the man who has known Christ and
calls himself a Christian. The latter cannot be excused if he
uses violence for his own ends.* So, too, the capitalist or the
colonialist who exploits and oppresses his fellow men, and
the government leader who uses police or military violence,
are to be radically condemned. Toward them, the church
can only take the attitude that St. Ambrose took toward

---

* Nowadays, almost everyone agrees that the use of any kind of violence
to protect "Christian values" or even Christians is unacceptable. Nevertheless, the tendency to use violence for these purposes recurs again and again.
To cite a present-day example: Many people were not at all surprised at the
report (in January, 1968; whether the report was correct I do not know)
that so noted a theologian as Helmut Thielicke had called on a number of
officer-candidates to prevent leftist students from disrupting the worship service at a Hamburg church by their demonstrations. Again, in Berlin, the faithful expelled R. Dutschke, who had wanted to discuss Vietnam during the
service. Christians must look upon such provocation as in the nature of persecution and must accept it calmly. They have no right to cope with it by
violence.

Theodore. On the other hand, the non-Christian—the one who, living under a tyrannous regime or in a society where, it seems, social injustice will never end, wants to kill the tyrant or destroy the society; the one who, exploited or degraded by a colonialist regime, wants to kill the oppressor; the man who, victimized by a racist society, wants to avenge by violence the indignities heaped upon him—all these, along with their violence, their hatred, their folly, must be accepted by those of us who are Christians. We know that they will only unleash violence, that they will solve no problems and will not bring in a better world; that such elements will appear, again and again, in a world of slavery and fear. But we cannot condemn these people. We must understand that when a man considers violence the only resort left him, when he sees it, not as a remedy and the harbinger of a new day, but as at least an indictment of the old, unjust order, when he thinks of violence as a way of affirming his outraged human dignity (his pride!)—in all these cases he is yielding to a normal urge, he is being natural, he is, though he is outside the law, at least being truthful.

For after all, there is no need to deny that violence has its virtues. It can bring about the disorder that is necessary when the established order is only a sanctimonious injustice, therefore condemnable and condemned. Within the system or necessities, violence may be a valid means. When the social order has turned into a moralistic, conformist system, a hypocritical humanism, then it is (socially) good that violence should crush the lie. Here Sorel is right. When the humanistic camouflage conceals terrorism (e.g., in the system of human and public relations, Training Within Industry, etc.), then violence is beneficial as a means of revealing what the true situation is. When the good will the superior so easily exhibits toward employees, students, children, etc., is only self-interest, a cover for his egoism and cowardice, then violence is normal. Violence is undoubtedly the only means for exploding façades, for exposing hypocrisy and hidden oppression for what they are; only violence reveals reality. It forces the "good boss" or the humanist politician to show himself in his true colors—as a savage exploiter or as an oppressor who does not hesitate to use violence when he meets resistance. It reveals that the superior is affable, kind, humane, understanding only so far as the inferior is servile, obedient, afraid, hard-working; otherwise, the superior turns ferocious.

Thus Christian realism and Christian radicalism must refuse to accept false solutions and appeasing compromises. Indeed the Christian must be watchful lest the oppressed party be deceived. For example, the Christian cannot accept the United States program of aid (including a state-guaranteed minimum income) for the blacks as a solution of the racial problem. In the long run a politics of aid—though it certainly relieves material want—degrades its beneficiaries morally, psychologically, and spiritually. The Christian must be on guard against that sort of thing. Thus—speaking as a Christian—I say that while I cannot call violence good, legitimate, and just, I find its use condonable (1) when a man is in despair and sees no other way out, or (2) when a hypocritically just and peaceful situation must be exposed for what it is in order to end it. But I must emphasize that in these cases, too, violence is of the "order of necessity," therefore contradictory to the Christian life, whose root is freedom. Moreover, I must emphasize that this understandable, acceptable, condonable violence may change quickly. Opposing an unjust order, creating a state of disorder out of which (depending on how fluid the situation is) renewal may issue—this is acceptable, provided that the users of violence do not pretend that they are creating order; what they are creating is one more injustice. The Christian simply cannot believe declarations that *this* violence will bring in a new order, a free society. There is just as much deceit here as in the order this violence is supposed to expose and oust. The hypocrisy of violence we spoke of rears its head again.

Moreover, violence cannot be accepted when it is made a factor in a strategy. We must sympathize with the man whose suffering explodes in violence, but we must refuse to countenance the one who considers violence a tool, a strategical tactic he is free to use at will. My objection to Che Guevara or Stokely Carmichael is that incitement to violence is (or was) a factor in their strategy—which is to say that they betray the people whose suffering drives them into anger and brutality. Thus human suffering and anger are turned into strings to operate marionettes, and these leaders reveal a hatred of humanity as deep as that of the leaders they oppose. It seems to me that a Christian cannot but sympathize with spontaneous violence. But calculated violence, violence incited as part of a strategy, is in no respect different from the violence of the general who orders his soldiers to their death and in the same breath praises them for their patriotism, etc. This is the lesson that Lenin taught us.

Now a problem arises as regards the violence the Christian finds understandable and acceptable: what should his relation to it be? Let me repeat what I said above—that the Christian cannot participate in a movement that makes violence and men's anger a factor in its strategy; nor can he credit an ideology that promises to establish a new order through violence. This said, the problem remains. It is true that where man is exploited, crushed, degraded by man, the Christian can neither avoid involvement by escape into the realm of spiritual values, nor side by default with the dominating party (as he has done so often in the course of history). Necessarily, in virtue of the calling to which Christ has called him, in virtue of the Lord's example, in virtue of the order of love, he is on the side of the little people, the poor. His place in the world is there—the only place the way of love leads to. Even if he does not deliberately choose this place, he is there, because his communion with Jesus Christ is communion with the Poor One who knew total poverty, total injustice, total violence. But when the Christian consciously keeps faith with his Lord, he is led to the least of these, the brethren of the Lord, and to the Lord himself (Matthew 25:40 ff.). However, can he therefore join those brethren in all their actions and demonstrations? Can he take the way of violence—which is the way of hatred—with them and for them? Can he participate in violence when it is what I have described as "understandable" violence? This last is the step too many Christians have taken of late. And in this connection I have three things to say.

If the Christian, because of his solidarity with the poor and the oppressed, joins their movement of redress, stands with them in their revolt, he may never use violence himself nor even unreservedly condone their violence. The Christian may not commit murder or arson even to defend the poor. Moreover, he must be on guard against creating the impression that his presence in the movement gives it a kind of moral guarantee. "The Christians are on our side" is interpreted as "God is on our side." It seems to me that, though there is some confusion about it, the case of Camilo Torres is in point here. Torres, readers will remember, was the Colombian priest who, seeing the terrible misery of his country's peasants and workers, became convinced that there was only one remedy for it, namely, the guerrilla movement. So he joined the guerrillas. But he could not participate in their

violence; he could only meet death at their side.* Giving
his life was his way of witnessing to Christ's presence among
the poor and the afflicted. Undoubtedly, his was a noble
and profound attitude. But I cannot say that it exemplifies
Christian truth, for violence was directly involved here.
Moreover, in such a case the Christian becomes a propaganda factor and the "good conscience" of men who have
no hope in Jesus Christ.† The only lesson to be drawn here
is that Christians who share the suffering of men must bear
witness to our Lord and Savior Jesus Christ in the worst and
most dangerous situations. It is good and necessary that
testimony to Jesus Christ be given among the guerrillas; but
this is the only justification for a Christian's presence in such
company, even if his presence is an act of heroism.

It may, however, happen that the Christian himself uses
violence. He has indeed often done so in the course of history. Oddly enough, all today's preachers of violence seem
unable to grasp the fact that they are comformists. They are
like the preachers of the Crusades, except that the crusade
they promote with their sermons on revolutionary violence is
the inverse of the old Crusades. Centuries ago, it was usually
(not always) the leaders who initiated violent movements
in the name of the faith; today the violent movement attacks
the leaders. Centuries ago, the purpose of the Crusade was
to gain possession of the holy places—a matter of piety; to-

---

* I know that there are conflicting views about Torres. Some consider him
a saint, who never bore arms and died without defending himself. Others
insist that he left the priesthood, became a regular guerrilla, and died with
his gun in his hand. These conflicting judgments show how confusing and
ambiguous Christian witness of that kind is, even when it is given with a pure
conscience.

† I am well aware that I shall be told that to do nothing is to condone the
violence of the oppressors!

day, the purpose is social. Save for these two differences
(which are not as important as they might seem), the old
and new movements are exactly the same, and so is the attitude of Christians with respect to them.

Be that as it may, his being a revolutionary (and, as I have
said, I believe that Christianity is profoundly revolutionary), his participation in the suffering of men, may lead a
Christian to use violence. He would do so during a revolution, just as millions of Christians did so during the world
wars. The point here is not that this is unacceptable, condemnable. The important thing is that, when he uses violence, the Christian knows very well that he is doing wrong,
is sinning against the God of Love, and (even if only in appearance) is increasing the world's disorder. He cannot conscientiously use violence in defense of the revolution of the
poor, cannot believe that the violence he commits is in conformity with the divine will and the divine order. The only
thing he can do is to admit that he is acting so out of his own
fears and emotions (not to defend oneself in battle is difficult, more difficult than to accept a death sentence calmly);
or else he can say that he is fighting *for* others, not to save his
own life. To say that, however, is to recognize that violence is
a necessity. In a revolution or a resistance movement, for instance, there are things that cannot be evaded, that have to
be done; violence must be used—it is a necessity. But in
such a situation the Christian must realize that he has fallen
back into the realm of necessity; that is, he is no longer the
free man God wills and redeemed at great cost. He is no
longer a man conformed to God, no longer a witness to
truth. Of course, he can say that he is only a man among men
—but that is not at all the calling to which God has called
him. He is once more traveling the rutted roads of this god-
less world. To be sure, the Bible tells of a great many men
who "made history," but these were not the men God

wished them to be. To fight even the worst of men is still to
fight a man, a potential image of God.

Thus violence can never be justified or acceptable before
God. The Christian can only admit humbly that he could
not do otherwise, that he took the easy way and yielded to
necessity and the pressures of the world. That is why the
Christian, even when he permits himself to use violence in
what he considers the best of causes, cannot either feel or
say that he is justified; he can only confess that he is a sinner, submit to God's judgment, and hope for God's grace
and forgiveness.

If I seem to be overstressing a point that is obvious and
banal, it is because I know some "violent Christians" who do
not at all take the attitude described above. Indeed, they are
so convinced of the justice of their cause that they are quite
pleased with themselves for being on the "right side."
Whereas, in face of the tragic problem of violence, the first
truth to be discerned is that, whatever side he takes, the
Christian can never have an easy conscience and never feel
that he is pursuing the way of truth.

Now let me offer a criterion. If the Christian joins a violent
movement to defend the oppressed (not to defend some political aim) he is like a foreign body in the midst of those
partisans (whether they be partisans of order or of revolution). For them, he is a kind of permanent bad conscience,
a reminder of something else, a witness to the Wholly
Other. His presence implies that their (and his) undertaking
is of a relative character. Moreover, he might change camps.

I say that the Christian *must* change camps once his
friends have won; that is, when in the aftermath of its victory the revolutionary party assumes power; for the party
will immediately begin to oppress the former oppressors.
This is the way things regularly go. I saw it in the case of the

French resistance to the Nazis. Therefore, if a Christian's participation in a violent movement was *truly* prompted by his concern for the poor, the oppressed, and the disinherited, *he must now change camps.* He must move to the side of the erstwhile "enemies"—the capitalists, the bourgeoisie, the collaborators, the Nazis, etc.—because they are now the victims, they are now the poor and the humiliated. Taking their part shows that his earlier involvement was authentic, that the reasons he gave for his participation in the violent movement were the true reasons. But if he stays on the side of the victors, he admits in effect that he was not really concerned for the poor and the oppressed in the first place. His insistence that he wanted to demonstrate his Christianity by serving men was a lie; his protest that he joined the violent movement in self-defense, because no other way was open to him, was also a lie. All his protests and declarations were a lie, a deceit, a hypocrisy. It is painful for me to pronounce this judgment on the multitude of Christians who sided with the National Liberation Front during the Algerian war. But after the war they were utterly indifferent to the fate of the *harkis*, the *pieds noirs*, and the Algerians oppressed by the new government. Therefore, their partisanship for the National Liberation Front was prompted by political views, by doctrinal or intellectual considerations, or—in most cases— simply by propaganda. Nothing in all this was, strictly speaking, Christian. And to cite Christian motivations in order to justify oneself in one's own eyes and the world's is to augment the evil. I must confess that considerable experience has taught me to be highly suspicious of Christian proponents of violence who appeal to such motivations.

I have tried to show that, while violence is inevitable and belongs to the order of necessity, this fact does not legitimize it in the sight of God; that indeed violence is contrary to the life in Christ to which we are called. Therefore, as Christians, we must firmly refuse to accept whatever justifications of violence are advanced; and in particular we must reject all attempts to justify violence on Christian grounds. Let me say once more that this applies to the violence of the powerful, of the capitalist, the colonialist and the state, as well as to the violence of the oppressed. I even say that it is not so much violence itself as justification of violence that is unacceptable to Christian faith. Violence as such, on the animal level, is the direct expression of our nature as animals; it certainly shows that we live in a state of sin—but that is nothing new. But any attempt to justify violence (by emotional considerations, by a doctrine, a theology, etc.) is a supplementary perversion of fallen nature at the hands of man. Remember Jesus' accusations against the Pharisees. He did not reprove them for doing the works of the law—on the contrary. What he attacked was their belief that their doing these works proved them *just,* their complacent conviction that their self-justifications were true.

Thus we as Christians are obliged on the one hand to attack all justifications for the use of violence, and on the other to refuse to provide Christian justifications. This second point ought to be, but is no longer, self-evident. Hence we are led to conclude that today's theologians of violence are pharisees, terrible distorters of Christian truth. And *hence* we are led to conclude that these theologians, despite all their kind sentiments, are helping to imprison man in the infernal circle of violence, which he can break out of only when he fully understands that doing violence is evil in the sight of God. Father Maillard says that "God has taken sides, therefore we are involved; we cannot express our faith except through imperfect temporal means, our love must be embodied in terms of economics and politics"; and on the basis of these generalities he concludes that violence is the proper mode of Christian action today. But to say this is to justify, in a most fearful way, all that is worst in man's fallen condition. This is in fact a resurgence—in other terms and with other objectives in view—of the error always committed by Christians who intervene in the sphere of human actions to justify them and to testify that in the end man has good reason for doing what he does. This is what theology did for centuries, for the benefit of state and king. And it is rightly criticized today. But justifying the violence of the other party amounts to the same thing.

In their radical refusal to justify violence, Christians must not leave the smallest breach. In particular, they must not draw up generalized formulas that, though they are likely to be rather empty, authorize every kind of deviation. I have in mind a host of declarations by popes, by the World Council of Churches, by our synods. An example: "One of the most important goods of human societies is that their defense against unjust aggression is fully justified."* Such a statement would justify all Hitler's and Stalin's enterprises from a Christian point of view. Formulas of this sort are dangerous because they have no concrete meaning. Moreover, they open a breach for the benefit of proponents of violence.

So, if a Christian feels that he must participate in a violent movement (or in a war!) let him do so discerningly. He ought to be the one who, even as he acts with the others, proclaims the injustice and the unacceptability of what he and they are doing. He ought to be the mirror of truth in which his comrades perceive the horror of their action. He ought to be the conscience of the movement; the one who, in behalf

---

* Christmas Message of Pope Pius XII, 1948. I cite this passage in order to show that the encyclical *Populorum progressio* is not so very novel!

of his unbelieving comrades, repents, bears humiliation, and prays to the Lord; the one who restrains man from glorifying himself for the evil he does.

And, mind, this is the only way open to the Christian. For him to condemn the violence of the "enemy" is useless, senseless, wide of the mark. For a Christian "of the left" to condemn the violence of the capitalists and the fascists, or for a Christian capitalist to condemn the violence of the workers or the guerrillas, is irrelevant. What is important is that the leftist Christian, for all his solidarity and sense of community with his comrades, should bring into his and their movement a critique of the violence they are using. Likewise as to the Christian capitalist. Let him say: "Yes, we exploit and oppress, we cannot do otherwise, but we are condemned by God for doing so, and we suffer."

Not only is this the one way a Christian caught in the toils of violence can witness to Jesus Christ; it entails concrete consequences of a very real kind. Let me mention two. First, as to physical violence: men are not directly and constantly prompted to use physical violence. To be sure, there are those who yield to "visceral" hatred and are ready to kill. But situations of raw violence are rare. Almost always, it is the conviction that "I am right" or "my cause is the cause of justice" that triggers violence. That is, the moment a value or an ideal is introduced, the moment motivations for fighting are advanced—in other words, the moment propaganda does its work—violence is unleashed. And violence can be reduced by countering this propaganda. For when a man is not quite sure of the virtue of his cause he hesitates to kill. So exposing the reality of violence as an animal reaction, as a "necessity," is automatically to reduce the use of violence. That is why Christians who side with the oppressed and justify violence in their behalf cannot, for all their good will and their seeming charity, be counted among the meek, nor among the merciful, nor among the peacemakers, nor yet among those who hunger and thirst for justice.

But to look at the matter from another angle: who will deny that a refusal on the part of the exploiters and the established powers and authorities to justify violence would be of unimaginable importance? Practically speaking, propaganda's only and invariable aim is to furnish justifications. To take away a government's (or a capitalist's) good conscience is to take away its power to use violence, because it is to take away its legitimacy. To induce a government (or a capitalist) to see its action as simple brute violence is to induce it to hesitate to use violence. But here again this cannot happen unless the question comes from within—unless the government official will not allow himself to evade it by saying, "Of course, he says that because he is a communist." The question must come from the very heart of the political and economic system. The Christian who, having accepted the communist regime in the U.S.S.R., protests the violence of that regime, should be "all things to all men"—not to show that a Christian will acquiesce in anything whatever, but to lead some of his compatriots to Christ; that is, in this connection, lead them to renounce violence. And if the man of power, the capitalist, and the colonialist go on using violence, their violence will be seen for what it is.

There was a great difference between the assassination of Malcolm X and that of Martin Luther King. Malcolm X preached only violence and hate, and hate and violence made answer—to no one's surprise. This assassination confirmed the argument that our society is based on the correspondence between hate and violence. But the death of Martin Luther King stunned the world. It was, after all, not normal for violence to be done him. In his assassination, hate showed its true face. King's murderers only succeeded in strengthening opinion against racism and apartheid. Thereafter, greater efforts were made to remedy the plight of the blacks.*

Two important facts must be taken into account here: a government's need to have a good conscience, and the influence of public opinion. It is not astonishing that, in a society like ours, governments do not employ all the means at their disposal unless they can do so conscientiously. The means are so overwhelming and destructive that those who use them must be sure that they are doing right. The Christian must attack an unjust regime not with arms but on the score of its legitimacy, its psychological and moral validity. He must attack the conscience of the regime's supporters. To be sure, this may take much time and may cost Christians dear. There will be no lightning-swift advances, no spectacular progress to bring glory on the Christians. Yet this is truly the only way open to them. When through their implacable meekness and their steady witness they succeed in demolishing the justifications a regime puts forward, the regime is forced to revise its policies. In the United States, it was thanks to Martin Luther King, not to Malcolm X, that the position of the blacks was greatly improved. Likewise in Spain, once the Spanish Christians began to challenge the Francoist regime, that regime was forced to modify and moderate its methods. I am certainly not saying that "nonviolent action" in itself is effectual. I am saying that by demolishing a regime's moral justifications, Christian witness deals it a much severer blow than criminal or guerrilla action can deliver.

Moreover, in our society, public opinion carries great weight. While this book is not concerned with politics, I cite

* This is why I cannot accept the statement of Julia Hervé (the daughter of Richard Wright) that King was defeated. He was "defeated" only from a non-Christian, nonspiritual, tactical point of view that makes efficiency its standard of judgment.

two important examples of how politics is affected by public opinion. In Algeria, the French army practically liquidated the NLF and all but won militarily. But, on the one hand, French opinion had gradually turned against the Algerian war and no longer accepted the government's arguments. And, on the other hand, world opinion, led by the U.S.A. and the U.S.S.R. (for once cooperating), was hostile to France. Therefore, in spite of its military victory, France had to accept defeat. The same kind of thing seems to be happening in regard to the Vietnam war. Militarily, America has probably already won. But world opinion is against her, and in the United States itself there is strong opposition (though American opinion on Vietnam is not as violent as French opinion on Algeria was in 1960). So the United States will have to yield. Events of this kind both prompt and confirm my contention that the refusal of Christians to condone an unjust regime will, in time, work powerfully.

CHRISTIAN RADICALISM

Necessarily, however, the effectualness of this approach depends on what I shall call Christian radicalism.* That is, if the Christian is to contend against violence (whatever its source), he will have to be absolutely intransigent, he will have to refuse to be conciliated. The Christian faith implies rejection and condemnation of both revolutionary violence and the violence of the established powers. "Thou shalt not kill" (as Jesus explained it) is to be considered not a law but a guiding principle in accomplishing the supreme task

* To obviate all misunderstanding, I must explain that I am using this term in the sense frequently given it by Anglo-Saxon theologians, who see "radicalism" as rooted in the tradition (Bishop Robinson, the death-of-God theologians). Here I mean by it that Christianity must be accepted in its revealed totality—accepted absolutely, intransigently, without cultural or philosophical or any other kind of accommodation or adaptation.

of man. It is when he is guided by those four words that man is man. In our materialistic times, man is identified as *homo faber*—which means that it is his use of tools, his utilization of wóod and stone, that differentiates him from the animals; that it is his practical reason, his doing, that marks him as man. I say that these are not at all the distinguishing characteristics. To some degree, animals know how to make use of things, and sometimes even employ artificial means (the monkey and the stick). What differentiates man radically from all other animals is this "Thou shalt not kill." For to say that is to flout the natural course of events. The animal kills what it needs to; killing is no problem for it at all. Nature is the power to kill. Slaughter is the basis for the development of life. But when he says "Thou shalt not kill," man affirms that he is different from animals, that he has embarked on a new course—in short, that he has found himself as man. "Thou shalt not kill" expresses the true being of man. All the demands implied in these words—faith in Jesus Christ, love of enemy, the overcoming of evil by love—must be affirmed, taught and lived with the most absolute intransigence. There can be no accommodation. The Christianity that accommodates itself to the culture in the belief that it will thus make itself more acceptable and better understood, and more authentically in touch with humanity—this is not a half-Christianity; it is a total denial of Christianity. Once Christianity gives way to accommodation or humanistic interpretation, the revelation is gone. Christian faith is radical, decisive like the very word of God, or else it is nothing.

Now, it is precisely a lack or a toning down of radicalism that characterizes the modern theological orientation (as it has so often characterized other theologies in the course of church history). Paul Tillich's theology of culture, Rudolf Bultmann's demythologization, today's death-of-God theology are all adaptations of Christianity to what is conceived of as the nature of man and modern society. It is very important for us to understand that every such effort, however intelligent, radically attacks the Lordship of Jesus Christ by removing its content and its power. This is not a matter of interpreting reality in a new way, giving it a new content, etc. Such accommodation robs the gospel of its radicalism and consequently renders the Christian powerless in the struggle against violence. To seek conciliation with the world is to cut off the gospel's roots. This, of course, assured Catholicism's worldly success—at the cost of its authenticity. Thus Catholicism was the great justifier first of feudal society, then of monarchy; and today, in exactly *the same* fashion, it justifies revolution. To seek a "balanced" conception of violence—to attempt to reconcile "effective love for the enemy" with "defense of rights," or to decide under what conditions armed insurrection is legitimate (for example, when the damage resulting from violence will be no worse than the damage being done by or through the current system—but as we have seen, this position is untenable), or to carry on any other such casuistry—this is to break with Christianity. Christians ought to understand clearly that Christianity has *nothing* to say in regard to this sort of thing.

But I know infallibly that at this point I shall be asked: This intransigent Christian radicalism of yours, doesn't it really mean withdrawal from the world? That, of course, is the great objection violent Christians always raise. They advance two arguments. The first is based on Charles Péguy's statement: "People who insist on keeping their hands clean are likely to find themselves without hands." Involvement in the world means getting dirty hands—that is, adjusting to the world. The intransigently Christian life can be lived only apart from the world. Christian radicalism is an abstraction that inhibits people from being involved with life because life is unclean. Though it looks like ascetic abstinence, this refusal to become involved is a flight from reality.

The second argument: Radical Christianity applies to the individual, and the individual is insignificant and ineffectual. Would the conversion of this rich man or that head of state bring any change whatever in the conditions man lives under today? Would it solve the problem of the oppressed? According to Father Maillard, there is no connection between authentic brotherly love and the hypothetical conversion of the rich man who oppresses his fellow human beings.

Let me deal briefly with these arguments. As to the first of them: To reject radical Christianity in order to plunge into action may be the thing for people who have a passion for action, but it is to reject Christianity itself. I have nothing against the person who prefers to take the way of politics, big business, science, revolution, technology, etc. Only, let him not pretend that he is thus witnessing to Christian truth. That much honesty can be demanded of him. Moreover, the idea that Christian radicalism inhibits action is utterly false. It calls for action—but of *another kind*. Certainly it inhibits the action of the capitalist bent on conquering new markets, the action of the guerrillas, etc. But it does require action. However, because Christianity is the revelation of the Wholly Other, that action must be different, specific, singular, incommensurable with political or corporate methods of action. Those who think that technological or political action is the only kind there is are, of course, free to go on thinking so. The worse for them. In any case, it is not by aligning Christianity with those sociological forms that the specific form Christian action should take today will be discovered.

The second argument must be taken very seriously, for (as so often happens nowadays) it casts doubt on certain Christian beliefs, namely, that we must preach the gospel so that men may be converted; that the purpose of preaching the gospel is neither to reform society nor to increase justice, but simply to convert men to their Lord Jesus Christ. In spite of all the current talk about "social Christianity," etc., an unbiased and unprejudiced reading of the Bible shows that converting men to their Lord is the work Christians are called to do. I do not have room here to develop the argument against "Christian-collective" systems (especially those whose proponents point to the primacy of the kingdom of God and interpret the kingdom in collective, social terms). I have only two things to say.

First, according to Father Maillard (referred to above), the rich man is not our brother, he is our enemy; eliminating him is the only thing that matters. In spite of all its sentimentality about the "little people" who are our brothers, a declaration like this is—from the Christian point of view—radically lacking in truth.

Second, this diminishment of the Wholly Other who has been revealed to us, this recourse to violence and to political and economic methods to express Christianity, is an admission that faith in the possibility of God's radical intervention, faith in the Holy Spirit, has been lost. Obviously, God intervenes radically only in response to a radical attitude on the part of the believer—radical not in regard to political means but in regard to faith; and the believer who is radical in his faith has rejected all means other than those of faith. The appeal to and use of violence in Christian action increase in exact proportion to the decrease in faith.* We are told that the Christian cannot take refuge in contemplation or pious

* Mind, I am saying neither that all human means of action are to be condemned nor that we should sit idly and await God's action. But the use of violence implies total confidence on the part of the user that it is justified—and this confidence is a crime against God. For example, I am taken aback by the following statement by Don Helder Camara, who otherwise is so worthy of regard: "We shall win [the revolutionary struggle] by creating widespread good will for our cause; or we shall lose all, and then *nothing can be saved.*" How can a Christian say that? Is there any other salvation than salvation in Christ? Does defeat on the socio-political level imperil that salvation?

prayers, that praying does not mean waiting passively for God to act on our behalf; that, on the contrary, praying means that we *too* must act. All of which is perfectly true. But then some people go to the other extreme and insist that we must do everything ourselves—"Help yourself (and, possibly, heaven will help you)!" Thus to stress human means—usually including violence—is in effect to stake everything on those means. If I think that I cannot reach others except by participating in their revolt, their anger and hatred; if I think that Christ's consolation is a deluding lie and reconciliation a hypocrisy, then I no longer believe that the coming kingdom is truly present (but it is a kingdom of *heaven*, not of earth), and I no longer believe in the Resurrection. And because in the depth of my heart I no longer believe these things—believe them confidently and unquestioningly, like the little child Jesus bade us imitate—I substitute for the Resurrection my mythological picture of it, and I decide that I shall have to build the kingdom on earth with my own hands. Because I do not believe these things, I think others cannot believe them either. Because I am not reconciled with my enemies (the rich, the powerful), I think I need not preach reconciliation. And because I believe that *everything* takes place on this earth (the rest being illusory), I think I can no longer proclaim the hope of Christ's *Return*. This unbelief (whose root, alas, is sociological, embedded in our culture) is the true root of Christian championship of violence. All the rest is illusion. Thus we face a decisive choice.

But, while Christian radicalism forbids participation in violence of any kind, it cannot counsel the poor and the oppressed to be submissive and accepting. I believe that, too often in history, Christians betrayed their faith by preaching resignation to the poor without at the same time constraining the rich to *serve* the poor. The Bible says that the Christian in an inferior position must not seek revenge, make demands, revolt; but in return the superior must become the servant of the inferior. Generally in preaching submission the church has forgotten the other side and thus has stood with the oppressors; it lent its moral authority to armed violence or to wealth and power. Naturally and justifiably, under such conditions the poor will reject the church. Today the church is biased in the other direction. It condones the struggle against the powerful and forgets that it should not exalt the pride of the poor.

But the main duty of the Christian nowadays is to urge the cause of the oppressed pacifically, to witness to their misery and to call for justice. The Christian should serve as intermediary or mediator between the powerful and the oppressed. He is the spokesman appointed by God for the oppressed. Those who are imprisoned need an advocate. Those who have been dismissed from the world's memory, who (in the terrible words of an Egyptian author) are "forgotten by God," need an intercessor. Was not that exactly the role Abraham played in behalf of Sodom? The Christian is necessarily on the side of the poor—not to incite them to revolution, hatred, and violence, but to plead their cause before the powerful and the authorities. If need be, he must break down the doors of the powerful and declare the claims of love and justice. This role is much more difficult and thankless than that of a guerrilla chieftain or a corporation head, and there is no glory in it. To gain entrance to a corporation head and insist on discussing his workers' plight with him is much more difficult than to march in a picket line, for it requires much more in the way of intelligence, ability, precise information, and strength of soul. But we must demand entrance to the powerful because, in virtue of representing the poor, we are ambassadors of Christ. I hold that in every situation of injustice and oppression, the Christian—who cannot deal with it by violence—must make himself completely a part of it as *representative of the victims*. The Christian has spiritual weapons. He must state the case, make it his own, compel the other to see it. He must—as we said above—create a climate of doubt, insecurity, and bad conscience. He lends his intelligence, his influence, his hands, and his face to the faceless mass that has no hands and no influence.

But all this implies that the Christian must meet two conditions. The first is, of course, that he accept Christian radicalism. He cannot represent the victims before the authorities unless he wears the armor of absolute intransigence. On the one hand, he must know how to "distance" himself from the poor who demand redress, in order to keep them from abandoning themselves to violence. It is not easy to resist the friends to whom you are close. The Christian must be solidly anchored lest he be swept along by the sociological current. On the other hand, he must remember that contact with the powerful always involves the danger of corruption. This corporation head, or that minister of state, is so "understanding," so "ready to talk," so full of "good will" that it is hard to be blunt about the needs and claims of the poor. Socialist and trade-union leaders know all about this kind of thing. As they carry on "dialogue" with the enemy, they find themselves being less and less violent and uncompromising. If the Christian acts as mediator or advocate, as representative of the poor, it is not to get little concessions or to conciliate points of view or to harmonize opposing interests; no, it is to plead the cause of absolute misery before absolute power (power is always absolute!), and to do this in a spirit of imperturbably calm and loving intransigence, without animosity or violence. He must not compromise even on the smallest point (as Moses could not compromise with Pharaoh), for he does not represent himself but is sent by God. And his faith should render him proof against threats, corruption, amiability, the proffer of honors. But it is only Christian radicalism that can make him such a mediator. Lest he allow himself to incline toward one side or the other, he must first and last represent the total claim of Christ. And because it means faith in *this* Lord, that radicalism leads the Christian to comprehend all situations fully (including the situation of the corporation head or the statesman—"I am become all things to all men"), and also to love his adversaries as he loves his friends. That radicalism guarantees that he will see all sides—and this makes it possible for him to take the role of mediator. But, some will say, this is utopian! No. It is an expression of the faith. And if we do not believe that the Lord in whom we trust can open the mouth of the dumb and move mountains, we have simply abandoned Christianity completely.

The second condition: The Christian must be the spokesman for those who are *really* poor and forgotten. I must say (and I want readers to be absolutely clear about this) that all the political and social movements which Christian friends of mine have joined precisely because they wanted to help the poor—that these movements very rarely show a concern to seek out, to find, to help the *really* poor. Many Christians participate in such movements only after others have called attention to this or that terrible situation, or after the struggle is three-quarters won. Christians specialize in joining struggles that are virtually over and in championing those of the poor who already have millions of champions. Which is to say that Christians are very susceptible to propaganda. In the great majority of cases, indeed in all the cases I know (Martin Luther King is the one exception), Christians step into line in response to vast propaganda campaigns, launched by others, for this or that group of the "poor"—for

example, the Algerians of the National Liberation Front, the
North Vietnamese, the proletariat.

Here two questions arise. First, when a group is defended
by world opinion, by a powerful organization, by the world's
strongest nations (the U.S.S.R, China), can it then be said
—even if they *still* suffer terribly—that these people are truly
abandoned and forgotten? Second, since in such cases Christians merely add their voices to a chorus that is already fully
staffed, since they bring to it nothing new (that is, nothing
Christian) and simply string along on the path cut by others
(chiefly, the path of violence)—can it then be said that their
participation has any value? I say it does not. I say
that, alerted by vast propaganda campaigns, they have
leaped to the defense of people who are not really the "poor"
Matthew 25 speaks about. In an earlier chapter, I mentioned
the Biafrans, the Sudanese, the Khurds, the Tibetans. I have
heard no Christian voice raised in their behalf.* That is because there has been no great propaganda in their favor. For
every victim of the Vietnam war, ten Biafrans, Tibetans, etc.,
have been slaughtered or atrociously tortured. But Christians are not interested. Most often, Christians who plunge
into "peace campaigns" do so for political reasons, not for
reasons of faith. And politically speaking the Khurds, the
Biafrans, etc., are not "interesting." A Christian who is authentically concerned for the poor must withdraw at once
from a movement that counts its adherents in millions.

The same kind of thing happens as regards individuals.
The "Debray case" was widely publicized all over the world;
so Christians—along with millions of others—rushed to
Debray's defense. But in 1963 a young woman named Melle
Cleziou, an agricultural engineer in Algeria, took part in a
maquis movement against Ben Bella and was arrested. Some
of her colleagues reported her case, but nobody was inter-

---

* As of this writing, late spring, 1968.

ested. She disappeared and is probably dead. Again, no Christian was interested. Or let me cite an example from the U.S.A. The problem of the Negroes is undoubtedly very important there, but today the world supports their cause. I should like to see Christians concern themselves for the Puerto Ricans in New York and the "wetbacks" in the Southwest, rather than for the blacks. The Puerto Ricans and the wetbacks are more truly oppressed, lost, forgotten. Of course I shall be told, "But we don't know anything about them." Exactly! If it is truly the task of Christians to play the role of spokesman for the oppressed, witness for the forgotten, then they must be so concerned about human misery that they take pains to discover the really lost before it is too late. "Too late" because they are dead, as in the case of Melle Cleziou (and this will perhaps soon be the case of the Sudanese and the Biafrans, who are in danger of vanishing altogether); or because they are so unjustly and hatefully oppressed that their own hatred breaks out in revolt (as in the case of the American blacks). If Christians have a prophetic vocation, they will fulfill it today by speaking out in behalf of those whom nobody knows but whom Christians can learn to know because the Holy Spirit guides them. It is true that the Spirit should have given us up long ago, so invariably do we fall for propaganda!

One thing, however, is sure: unless Christians fulfill their prophetic role, unless they become the advocates and defenders of the truly poor, witness to their misery, then, infallibly, violence will suddenly break out. In one way or other "their blood cries to heaven," and violence will seem the only way out. It will be too late to try to calm them and create harmony. Martin Luther King probably came ten years too late for the black Americans; the roots of violence had already gone deep. So, instead of listening to the fomenters of violence, Christians ought to repent for having been too late. For if the time comes when despair sees violence as the only possible way, it is because Christians were not what they should have been. *If violence is unleashed anywhere at all, the Christians are always to blame.* This is the criterion, as it were, of our confession of sin. Always, it is because Christians have not been concerned for the poor, have not defended the cause of the poor before the powerful, have not unswervingly fought the fight for justice, that violence breaks out. Once violence is there, it is too late. And then Christians cannot try to redeem themselves and soothe their conscience by participating in violence.

I have tried to show clearly in what respect the action of the Christian must be specific, unique. This entails important consequences. Christians must not require others to act *as if* they were Christians, as if they held a Christian ethic. I cannot develop this theme here. Readers will find fuller treatment of it in other of my books.* If an ethic is Christian, it is a product of the faith, acceptable and possible only to faith. Therefore it is literally impossible to require others to obey that ethic—to demand that they live as if they were Christians, even though they do not possess the faith. To demand that would be to set up for them objectives they can neither understand nor attain. On the other hand, an ethic that would be equally valid for Christians and for non-Christians—in virtue of its not being specifically Christian—would necessarily be a non-Christian ethic (such as John A. T. Robinson presents in his rather mediocre *Christian Morals Today*). But this would be to say that there is no such thing as specifically Christian action, therefore that there is no possible way of incarnating the faith.† In so far as

* *Le vouloir et le faire; Introduction à l'éthique* (Geneva: Labor & Fides, 1964).

† Except (according to Robinson) "love." But "love" means nothing concrete, it is empty, muddled. It reminds one of Christianity's worst days of sentimental love.

I firmly believe that faith in Jesus Christ requires action of a specific, unique, singular kind, I must admit that the counsels on violence issuing from the faith are addressed to faith, therefore can have no meaning for those who do not believe that Jesus Christ is Lord. For example, we cannot expect non-Christians to bear oppression and injustice as we ought to bear them. So we cannot do as the church has so often done: remind the world's oppressed (very few of whom are Christians) of their "Christian duty" to submit and practice resignation.

To us, this "Christian duty" is native. We Christians must submit and bear unjust suffering; "for if when you do right and suffer for it you take it patiently, you have God's approval" (I Peter 2:20). But we cannot make this a law for all men. We must accept injustice *ourselves*, but we can neither require others to bear it patiently nor serve as example for them, nor yet bear their suffering for them. That is to say, we cannot tolerate the injustice done others. The Christian's first act of nonviolence is that he refrain from asking others to live as if they were Christians. When violence is in question, it is not our business to lecture them and urge them to be nonviolent. Of course—as I have said again and again— we cannot participate in violence, any more than we can participate in oppression and injustice. But if (as I said above) we must try to solve a bad situation before it becomes worse and reaches the stage where violence is on hand, it will do no good to urge non-Christians not to use violence. In whose name, or why? In any undertaking, non-Christians necessarily act out of their human motives. They pursue their own interests at any cost, or they try to dominate others; or they may tend to be cruel and so they create inhumane situations; or they are obsessed with power and pride; etc. If we believe that *Jesus Christ alone* is Lord and Savior, then we should not be astonished or scandalized when such things happen. Rather, we should marvel when such things do *not* happen, when through human means a kind of order and peace and justice reigns; for this is the miracle, and we should thank and praise God for it, and also this or that man.

Thus if we are serious we must accept the fact that men plunge into violence, and we must try to limit the effects and remedy the causes of that violence. But we shall not be able to deter men from violence. While Christians can never participate in violence for any reason whatever, it is not up to them to condemn those who use it. From this point of view, the attitude of Rap Brown and Stokely Carmichael is completely honest. They had been Christians, but they chose violence and *therefore* rejected Christianity. "My people, my fellow blacks, are my religion. I am not a Christian. Even if Christ were black, Christianity is still something Western. Every time blacks are killed a priest is on hand with his cross. We don't need priests and crosses. We need to answer killing with killing. . . . Many of us believed in God. But two years ago we were told that God was dead. Then we began to believe in ourselves. We have learned to kill by believing in ourselves, not by believing in God or Christianity." Thus Brown.* And Carmichael: "We've had more than enough of missionaries. We are no longer Christians. When the missionaries came to Africa, we had the land and they had the Bible. Now they have the land and we have the Bible." †

I find statements like these infinitely more serious and to my liking than the statements of Christians who try to justify the violence they preach. At least Brown and Carmichael are men who made a real choice, who did not even attempt

* *Nouvel observateur,* September 11, 1967.
† Conference at Havana, August 2, 1967.

a shabby reconciliation, and who saw clearly that violence is radically incompatible with faith in Jesus Christ. They chose violence; that was their privilege. All that a Christian could do would be truly to convert them to Jesus Christ. But certainly the Christian cannot hypocritically counsel them to renounce what they believe is the right way for them; nor can the Christian justify them with a theological benediction that they have been honest enough to refuse. Where they are concerned, we know at least where we are.

But now let me give a warning. If the Christian cannot demand, cannot even suggest, that non-Christians should act as though they were inspired by the Christian faith, he must take the same attitude toward the revolutionaries and toward the state. To demand that a non-Christian state should refrain from using violence is hypocrisy of the worst sort; for the Christian's position derives from the faith, and moreover he exercises no responsible political function. To ask a government not to use the police when revolutionary trouble is afoot, or not to use the army when the international situation is dangerous, is to ask the state to commit hara-kiri. A state responsible for maintaining order and defending the nation cannot accede to such a request. The intellectuals can play the game on their own terms; they hold no political office, they are outsiders; so it is easy for them with their high principles to decide what should be done. Christian honesty and Christian humility would prompt the question: "If I really were in that official's position, what would I risk doing?" And it is a well-known fact that the very intellectuals who criticize power so violently do no better than others once they themselves have arrived in places of power.

In the face of a non-Christian state, all the Christian can do is—not read it a moral lecture, not rail at it and demand the impossible; not these things. All the Christian can do is to remind the state that, though it be secularized and its

officials be atheists, it and they are *nevertheless* servants of
the Lord. Whether they know it or not, whether they like it
or not, they are servants of the Lord—*for the good.* And they
will have to render account to the Lord for the way they did
their service. Obviously the Christian's task is not a very
pleasant one. He is ridiculed, he is isolated from other political movements; he cannot howl with the wolves!

On the other hand, if a statesman, the president of the
republic, openly declares himself a Christian, then—on the
basis of his own faith—the total demands of the Christian
faith can be set before him. It ought to be possible to
tell President de Gaulle that his faith forbids the machiavel-
lianism, the cynicism, the contemptuousness, the political
realism that inspire all his decisions. It ought to be possible
to tell a President Johnson that his faith forbids any use
of violence and that the Crusades were never truly
an expression of the Christian faith. With and only with
these men, and only on the basis of *their* affirmation of faith,
could Christians and the church hold dialogue on matters
of this kind. But here, too, Christians *must* refrain from participating in mass movements. They must not join others
in passionate condemnation (or support), in the name of
fifty humanist motifs put forward by non-Christians, of such
a politics conducted by a statesman who calls himself Christian. The important thing is to make him see that he has to
draw the consequences of his faith; and perhaps he will
verify the fact that it is impossible to be a Christian and at
the same time to conduct a successful politics, which necessarily requires the use of some kind of violence.

THE VIOLENCE OF LOVE

After all, to say that Christianity forbids *all* violence is not
entirely correct. The Old Testament tells of a great many

violences, though the greatest care must be used in interpreting those passages.* In any case, there is such a thing as
spiritual violence, and we must try to understand it. Jesus is
the sign of contradiction. "I have not come to bring peace,
but a sword. . . . I came to cast fire upon the earth; and
would that it were already kindled! . . . The kingdom of
heaven is for the violent who seize it by force. . . . It is a
terrible thing to fall into the hands of the living God. . . . It
is not against flesh and blood that you must contend." Many
other passages speak of strife, contention, violence. But we
must be clear that this is not contention against flesh and
blood, but against the powers. It will not do to take this text
(as many take it) as referring exclusively to the individual
with his tendencies, his body, his sins. It has a collective reference also; it applies to the whole group. It is not against
flesh and blood that we must contend; that is, not against
whatever material, visible, concrete forces anyone can discern. How many moral and political systems have done so

* I give three brief examples. (1) The Hérem [i.e., The Ban; see Deu-
teronomy 2 and 7, Joshua 6, I Samuel 15]. Obviously these passages are not
to be taken as mandatory laws but as descriptions of an institution connected
with a certain culture, whose *significance* alone concerns us. This is intended
to mark the strict separation between the chosen people of God, who is holy,
and the peoples who worship false gods. The atrocious Hérem is intended to
keep the people from idolatry.

(2) The prophets speak against the rich, but they never incite the poor to
take justice into their own hands, to use violence. The prophets always pronounce God's judgment on the rich, they speak the word against the rich, but
at the same time they declare that justice is the Lord's and that trust must be
placed in him.

(3) Elijah slaughters the prophets of Baal. Three points must be empha-
sized here. It was not as a political or military leader, but as a prophet, and
only after a miracle had been performed (thus in a limited situation), that
Elijah did his violent deed. He was struggling against the powers, the idols,
the false gods, not contending for political justice or some human good. He
stood alone, not only against the state but against the people also. He was
working against the current. Only later did God reveal to him that some of
Israel's people had remained faithful.

on the moral and political levels; and in our day the contest
is carried on by socialism. All the others are fighting this battle. Humanly speaking, they have the wisdom and the capacity to create better (relatively better) institutions. But
what would be the use of the Incarnation, the Cross, the
Resurrection, if Christians were meant to be and to act just
like the others?

You are set aside for a more difficult and more profound
struggle—less visible, less exalting; and it will bring you no
glory. People will not understand what you are doing and
will not thank you for it. Indeed they will often think that
you are traitors. But the truth is that you stand at the center
of the battle, and that without your action the rest of it would
mean little. It was thus that Moses fought against Amalek.
While the people, led by Joshua, fought, killed and were
killed, Moses went to the top of the hill and held up his hand.
And the battle's issue depended on that hand, lifted in
blessing or lowered in bane—though the people did not directly perceive the relation between Moses' hand and the
fortunes of the battle (Exodus 17:8-13). It is because nonviolence and the violence of love are rooted in the life of
Christ that rational judgments of the work of Martin Luther
King are absolutely useless. To say, as did Malcolm X and
Julia Hervé, that "nonviolence is historically passé," is to utter nonsense. For their judgment arises from a basic inabil-
ity to understand, hence to cooperate with, those who use
the tactic of nonviolence as others use the tactic of violence.

To contend against the powers: I am quite familiar with
the traditional and present-day critics of the Bible who interpret this as a kind of magical talk, who say, for instance,
that Paul's *exousiai* inhabit a mythical world and that little
importance attaches to them. I shall say simply that this is the
position of the cultural and demythologizing schools of interpretation, which I consider altogether superficial. I re-

main convinced by Barth's and Cullmann's exegeses of the powers (which certainly are not to be assimilated to "angels," as these are popularly and simplistically conceived of; but this is exactly the error many biblical critics make!). In one of my books* I have tried to show that the Mammon Jesus speaks of in connection with money is one of these powers; and in another book† that even when one approaches phenomena like the state, money, sexuality, law from another angle, one arrives at the idea that behind these phenomena there is something that cannot be reduced to rational terms, something that suggests a deeper existence and is not altogether explicable on the human level. Well then, if we contend against the state or social injustice only on the human level, we shall, of course, bring about some apparent changes, but the basis will remain untouched and nothing decisive for humanity will be gained. The battle against injustice, etc., will not avail unless another battle is fought with and outside it, namely, the spiritual battle against what constitutes the "soul" of these material phenomena. Nevertheless, we should not therefore scorn or disregard the material battle. For example, in the racial conflict, how idle it is to talk about "integration of hearts" so long as millions of blacks are not integrated into economic life. Thus Christians must reject psychological integration and insist on the importance of economic integration; but their specific task is to carry on the spiritual battle against the demonism of racism.

For the powers are *incarnated* in very concrete forms, and their power is expressed in institutions or organizations. We cannot think of the battle as only a spiritual one. The *exousia* of the state is incarnated in a government, in the police force,

* *L'homme et l'argent* (Neuchâtel and Paris: Delachaux & Niestlé, 1954).
† *Le fondement théologique du droit*, 1948. English edition, *The Theological Foundation of Law* (New York: Doubleday, 1960; paperback, Seabury, 1969).

the army, and it is not enough to partake of the Lord's victory. The battle against these material powers certainly must be fought. We must neither forget it nor ignore it. But I might say that there is a kind of division of labor here. People generally join the material struggle out of their own volition, spontaneously. They are able to conduct these political or economic wars, and if need by they will do it by violent means. But the other war can be waged only by Christians, for they have received the revelation not only of God's love but also of the creation's profound reality. Only Christians can contend against the powers that are at the root of the problem. The state would be powerless and unimportant were it not for the something-more-than-itself that resides within it. And to contend against institutions or against the men who serve the institutions (the police, for instance) is useless. It is the heart of the problem that must be attacked. And Christians alone can do that—because the others know nothing about all this, and because only the Christians receive the power of the Holy Spirit and are required by God to do these things. I know the temptations! People will say: "The Christians keep the good part for themselves. They evade the hard, dangerous battle and stay calmly in their room and pray." Well, people who do not know what it is all about will talk like that. They will say: "The Christians are full of kind words. They insist that they are participating in our struggle, but they are careful not to get their hands dirty, and so they can keep a good conscience." Anyone who has never fought spiritually will agree.

But, as Rimbaud told us, "spiritual warfare is just as brutal as human warfare." We know what price Jesus paid for waging his battle spiritually. But this spiritual contest is concerned only with the incarnated powers. We are not called to fight against an abstract Satan lurking among the celestial spheres. The spiritual battle proclaimed by some mysticism or gnosis is a false one. The spiritual warfare we are summoned to is concerned with human realities—with injustice, oppression, authoritarianism, the domination of the state by money, the exaltation of sex or science, etc. This is the spiritual battle that is to be fought alongside the human battle against material phenomena. We cannot evade it. We are in fact those men's comrades in the struggle, though they do not know it. And Christian humility, patience, and nonviolence require us to bear with their derision and their accusations.

We are to wage the warfare of faith, our only weapons those Paul speaks of: prayer, the Word of God, the justice of God, the zeal with which the gospel of peace endows us,* the sword of the Spirit. . . . And if we think this is easy, it is because we know nothing about life in Christ, because we are so sunk in our materialistic culture that we have quite forgotten the meaning of God's work in us, quite forgotten what we are called to in the world. For to wield Paul's weapons is certainly not to live a smug, eventless life. The fight of faith demands sacrificing one's life, success, money, time, desires. In the United States, for instance, the fight of faith demands that the blacks be accepted totally, that they be granted full equality, and also—because they have been oppressed and insulted—that their arrogance, their insults, and their hatred be borne. The fight of faith is perfectly peaceable, for it is fought by applying the Lord's commandments. Humanly speaking, to fight thus is to fight nakedly and weakly, but it is precisely by fighting so that we strip bare and destroy the powers we are called to contend against.

---

* I consider "zeal" most particularly important; the term means military courage, such as characterized the Zealots. Paul expressly associates "zeal" with the Good News of Peace: we are to be zealous—that is, courageous like soldiers—for the peace which Jesus brought for all men, but which must be established on earth.

It is not by sequestering ourselves in our churches to say little prayers that we fight, but by changing human lives. And it is truly a *fight*—not only against our own passions and interests and desires, but against a power that can be changed only by means which are the opposite of its own. Jesus overcame the powers—of the state, the authorities, the rulers, the law, etc.—not by being more powerful than they but by surrendering himself even unto death.

Let me give a very simple example. How overcome the spiritual "power" of money? Not by accumulating more money, not by using money for good purposes, not by being just and fair in our dealings. The *law of money* is the law of accumulation, of buying and selling. That is why the only way to overcome the spiritual "power" of money is to give our money away, thus desacralizing it and freeing ourselves from its control. And these benefits accrue not only to us but to all men. To give away money is to win a victory over the spiritual power that oppresses us. There is an example of what the fight of faith means. It requires us to give ourselves and to use specific weapons that only Christians know of and are able to use.

But, as Rimbaud says, this fight involves violence—spiritual violence, the violence of love. For there is such a thing as the violence of love. It is not the violence of terror or coercion, but the violence that makes us intransigent toward ourselves and insistent in our demand that the other live— I might say, "that the other live in a manner worthy of God's image." For to live like that does not come naturally; indeed it is the result of a sort of antinature. But the other cannot be compelled to be fully man except in and through absolute love. If we believe in the truth of Christ's love, if that love accomplished all in order that we might live, we must go Christ's way. But we cannot cast the other aside, into nothingness, hatred, or death. And we cannot fall in with some sociological trend or conform to popular opinion. Compelling the other to live as man certainly does not mean having rights over him in any way, being his boss, his tutor, his guide, his counselor; it means urging him forward with the violence of a love that never seeks its own advantage, never seeks to possess or to dominate.

For we must not forget that there are two kinds of love: Eros, which seeks to possess and dominate, and Agape, which gives—gives itself, too. Contrary to a modern idea, Eros is not one of the legs of Agape. The Christians who preach violence in the name of love of the poor are disciples of Eros and no longer know the Agape of Christ. Only in the light of Jesus Christ's sacrifice of himself can man be compelled to live as man. In following the path appointed by Christ we show the other to himself. Camus understood this; he showed that there is a link between the victim and the executioner, showed how the victim can compel the executioner to become a man by recognizing his victim. Seeing the crucified Christ the Roman centurion said, "Certainly this man was innocent." Seeing Joan of Arc burned at the stake the English captain said, "We have burned a saint." At that moment they became men.

We must note when we speak of the violence of love that this love—affirmed, proclaimed, lived, attested by gentle signs—is a force that can cause great perturbation. I said above that the struggle against the powers is a secret and sometimes an invisible struggle; well, love is its visible form. Just apply the love Paul revealed to us, just try to obey the simple commandment "Thou shalt not kill," and you will create such confusion and trouble in the social body that this love becomes unacceptable. That is why theology has been trying for two thousand years to regulate things. Bishop Robinson recently explained that we naturally cannot apply the counsels of the Sermon on the Mount. These are only symbols, parables of love. Jesus was never interested in the conflicting demands inherent in every life situation. Very convenient, isn't it? But the truth is that willingness to apply these counsels of love strictly (not of course as if they were a law, a code, a set of rules) will turn human relations upside down and provoke harsh reactions in the body social. Let me remind readers of the extraordinary experience of Toyohiko Kagawa, who was undoubtedly an upsetter of people.

This violence of love is an expression of spiritual violence. Spiritual violence, however, is neither acceptable nor possible except on three conditions. First, it must reject all human means of winning a victory or registering effects. I should like to broadcast the innumerable Old Testament passages which tell how God opposed his people's use of "normal" means of settling conflicts—weapons, chariots, horsemen, alliances, diplomatic maneuvers, revolution (Jehu)—and bade them put their trust in the Lord's word and his faithfulness. This is radical spiritual violence. And God lets us choose. Paul also lets us choose. He tells us that he did not come "proclaiming the testimony of God in lofty words or wisdom," lest rhetoric and philosophy hide the power of the Spirit. I do not say that we are forbidden to employ human means. I say that when we do employ them (and we are not condemned for doing so!) we take away from the Word that has been entrusted to us all its force, its efficacity, its violence. We turn the Word into a sage dissertation, an explication, a morality of moderation. When we use political or revolutionary means, when we declare that violence will change the social system we are *thus* fighting in defense of the disinherited, our violence demolishes the spiritual power of prayer and bars the intervention of the Holy Spirit. Why? Because this is the logic of the whole revelation of God's action—in Abraham the disinherited wanderer, in Moses the stutterer, in David the weakling, in Jesus the Poor Man. Provided we reject human means, our spiritual intervention may become effectual spiritual violence. Of course, this involves risk. But if we do not take the risk, we can only take the middle way, and even if we plunge into armed, violent, extremist revolution, we are still among the lukewarm. I need hardly say that this is no brief for the traditional sanctimonious patter of the churches that have retreated into their piety, or for the mediocre, musty, introverted, and highly moral lives of many Christians, who are impervious to the violence of love and the power of the Spirit. It is only at a certain level of intensity, urgency, spiritual earnestness that the problem of this choice arises. And, as I said, the choice one makes is decisive, for only if it is the right one is spiritual action possible and spiritual violence legitimate.

Hence a second condition, consequent to the first. Spiritual violence and the violence of love totally exclude physical or psychological violence. Here the violence is that of the intervention of the Spirit of God. The Spirit will not intervene, will not rush in with explosive power, unless man leaves room—that is, unless man himself intervenes. It is precisely because in this fight the Christian has to play a role that no one else can fill—it is precisely for this reason that the Christian can accept no other role. He makes himself ridiculous when he tries to be a politician, a revolutionary, a guerrilla, a policeman, a general. Spiritual violence radically excludes both the physical violence and the participation in violent action that go with such roles. It is not authentic spiritual violence unless it is only *spiritual* violence. It plays its role of violence with, before and against God (the struggle of Abraham and Jacob) only when it refrains from any other violence. And this exclusion is required not only by the decision of God as recorded in the Scriptures, but also and to a greater degree, by the fact that the Christian can never consider violence the *ultima ratio*. We have seen all along that this is the argument regularly trotted out to justify violence. Violence, we are told, is legitimate when the situation is such that there is absolutely no other way out of it. The Christian can never entertain this idea of "last resort." He understands that for the others it may be so, because they place all their hopes in this world and the meaning of this world. But for the Christian, violence can be at most a second-last resort. Therefore it can never be justified in a Christian life, because it would be justified only by being really a last resort. The Christian knows only one last resort, and that is prayer, resort to God.

Please, let no one bring up again the inevitable and useless argument: "We must do what we pray for, we cannot ask for daily bread for ourselves without giving daily bread to others." I accept that as expressing a pastoral point of view and a serious attitude toward prayer. But that is not at all what prayer means. To say "Our Father" is to put oneself into God's hands, to submit to his decisions, to trust in his mercy—and to appeal the unjust judgments of men to the just judgment of God. No, the idea of violence as *ultima ratio* is intolerable, and for that reason (among other reasons) the Christian cannot take any part of it. It is precisely in the midst of violence that he must witness to another resort and another hope, just as serious, as efficacious, as dependable as activism. To be sure, if he does this where violence and revolution are rife, he will be laughed at or treated like a coward or an opium dealer. In our society, it is much more difficult to stand up for the truth than to go to Colombia and fight for justice or to join the Ku Klux Klan to quell the black uprising. But if the Christian does not bear witness to truth, he is just as hypocritical as his forefathers were when they used Christianity to justify commercial ventures or to support their social order. When some kind of sociopolitical activity is the important thing, faith in Christ is only a means.

Nowadays, for a Christian to say that violence (any kind of violence, whatever its origin and its aim) is the *ultima ratio* is to signalize his infidelity—and the primary meaning of that word is "absence of faith."

So we come to the third condition in relation to spiritual violence. If it is true spiritual violence, it is based on earnest faith—faith in the possibility of a miracle, in the Lordship of Jesus Christ, in the coming of the Kingdom through God's action, not ours; faith in *all* of the promise (for the promise must not be taken apart into bits and pieces, in the manner of the theologians of revolution). This is a faith that concerns not only the salvation of the believer; it concerns the others, the unbelievers; it carries them and takes responsibility for them; it is convinced that for these others, too, there is a truth, a hope greater than revolutionary action, even if this hope does not attach to the material side of life. All of which is to say that there is a real choice to be made here (and making it will surely be the heaviest burden placed upon the Christian who tries to live his faith). We cannot, by taking neither, play on both sides. But if we witness to spiritual violence before the others, we cannot go on living in material violence, living for ourselves, protecting our own interests or our society. The choice is between violence and the Resurrection. Faith in the Resurrection—which is the supreme spiritual violence because it is victory over the necessity of death—excludes the use of every other violence. And it is true that, the Resurrection being accomplished, we can and must proclaim consolation and reconciliation. For men today have much greater *need* of true consolation than of economic growth, of reconciliation than of appeals to hate and violence.

I know that by saying that I am prompting the accusation: "This kind of discourse is an attempt to divert the poor from revolution; this is the talk of a watchdog of capitalism and the bourgeois order." I know. I have two things to say in answer. First, no one can hold "this kind of discourse" unless (as we have seen) he is also and simultaneously acting as spokesman for the oppressed and attacking the unjust order with every nonviolent weapon. Second, even if such discourse were uttered by a liar using it to defend other interests (and I doubt that such a liar would use it), it would still be true.* Nevertheless, we Christians must always bear this accusation in mind, lest we speak such words lightly. We should accept it as an alert (sounded by the perspicacious non-Christian) that bids us be aware before God of what we can proclaim in truth to the poor in our midst. But we must also be thoroughly aware that when we, as Christians, hold a discourse on violence, it is our lack of faith that speaks.

The whole meaning of the violence of love is contained in Paul's word that evil is to be overcome with good (Romans 12: 17-21). This is a generalization of the Sermon on the Mount.† And it is important for us to understand that this

---

* The easy answer is that Marxist discourse can no longer be taken seriously because Stalin used it, and that no one can be a Marxist because Marxist discourse produced the worst of dictatorships.

† I think Father Régamey (*op. cit.*, pp. 108 ff.) is mistaken when (following the Catholic tradition that distinguishes between precepts and counsels) he says: "Love of enemies can degenerate into abdication and treason when it is understood as an absolute command . . . and this leads to disowning the order of love. The 'rigorists,' that is, those who hold that the Sermon on the Mount must be taken with radical seriousness—render obedience to God's command impossible." Then, Father Régamey says, the Christian turns away from it and, because he tried to make it absolute, annuls it. It must be recognized, he continues, that the way the Sermon on the Mount calls to is extraordinary (that is, not prescribed for all). He gives an example. The command against killing, he says, is based on the sacred character of human life (?), and "love your enemies" does not mean that the Lord forbids us "to yield to the inevitabilities to which human nature [?] is subject. In the various cases, we must as best we can strike a balance between effective love toward the assailant and defense of the right." In my opinion, this is a mistake. It is precisely the kind of toning down that is the source of all Christianity's weaknesses.

The Fight of Faith 173

sermon shows what the violence of love is. Paul says, "Do not let yourself be overcome by evil." This then is a fight—and not only spiritual, for Paul and the whole Bible are very realistic and see that evil is constantly incarnated. But to be overcome by evil does not mean that he who is overcome is weaker, inferior, beaten, eliminated; no, it means that he is led to play evil's game—to respond by using evil's means, to do evil. That is what it means to be overcome by evil, to respond to violence by violence. Paul bids us *overcome* evil with good, and this, too, is the imagery of contest. We are not to bend or yield before evil, nor to act like cowards or impotent weaklings: we are to overcome, to *surmount* evil, to go beyond it, to stand on a terrain that evil cannot reach, use weapons that evil cannot turn back on us, seek a victory that evil can never attain!

Choosing different means, seeking another kind of victory, renouncing the marks of victory—this is the only possible way of breaking the cha'n of violence, of rupturing the circle of fear and hate. I wou 1 have all Christians take to heart this word of Gandhi's: "Do not fear. He who fears, hates; he who hates, kills. Break your sword and throw it away, and fear will not touch you. I have been delivered from desire and from fear *so that I know* the power of God."* These words show that the way Christ appointed is open to all, that the victory of good over evil benefits not only Christians but non-Christians also. In other words, that if the Christian knows that the fight of faith promises *this* victory, it is not only his victory but others' too. If he sees that the others are obsessed by violence and can find no other way, he has to play another card with them and for them. How is it that, in the midst of the racial struggle going on in the United States today, so many white Christians leave to black Christians the

* Camille Drevet, *Pour connaître la pensée de Gandhi* (Paris, 1954), p. 129.

appanage of nonviolence? Why do they not take the way of repentance and conciliation in the face of black violence—repentance for the violences the whites committed in the past? Why, in the face of the black violence they provoked, do they not now seek peace *at any price*? It is only by love that is total, without defense, without reservation, love that does not calculate or bargain, that the white Christian will overcome the evil of revolution, arson, and looting. I make bold to say this even though I am not in the United States; I have lived through similar situations elsewhere.

Neither exaltation of power nor the search for vengeance will ever solve any human situation. In accepting death, Jesus Christ showed us the only possible way. We may refuse to take it. But we must realize that when we refuse we are left with one alternative—increasing the sum of evil in the world. And we ought to be honest and renounce all pretensions to the Christian faith. Surely we shall not use the suffering of the others whose side we take as an excuse for evading the only way that is open for faith. And if vengeance must be exacted, if a judgment, a condemnation must be pronounced, they are the Lord's alone. This holds on the social as well as on the individual level. To pretend to end exploitation by force is to eliminate the exploiter by violence, to exercise the judgment that is God's to exercise. For as we have seen throughout this investigation, there can be no use of violence without hate, without judgment, without abomination. Violence and revolution—let them continue! But without the presence and justification of Christians. This does not mean, however, that Christians are permitted to execrate or judge those who do take part in violence and revolution.

Will it be said then that the Christians are absent from the world? Curious that "presence in the world" should mean accepting the world's ways, means, objectives; should mean helping hate and evil to proliferate! Christians will be sufficiently and completely present in the world if they suffer with those who suffer, if they seek out with those sufferers the one way of salvation, if they bear witness before God and man to the consequences of injustice and the proclamation of love.

Index